CW01656410

SCREEN ADDICT

Parenting Success Stories
That Will Change
Your Life

SCREEN ADDICT

Parenting Success Stories That Will Change Your Life

MÜNÜR SHAH

RT PRESS

Screen Addict:
Parenting Success Stories That Will Change Your Life

First Print Edition

REBEL THERAPIES PRESS

Rebel Therapies Press is part of Rebel Therapies Limited whose registered address can be found at www.rebeltherapies.com

Copyright © Munur Shah 2024

First published in the United Kingdom by Rebel Therapies Press.

All rights reserved, including the right to reproduce this book or portions thereof in any form whatsoever. For information, address the publisher.

A CIP catalogue record is available from the British Library.

ISBN: 978-1-0685-5684-5

Front Cover and Interior Illustrations: Liliye Shah

Requests to publish work from this book should be sent to:
Munur@RebelTherapiesPress.com

PRESS

www.RebelTherapies.com

For Melanie,
Beker, and Liliye x

Table of Contents

Acknowledgements

I have many to thank for their support in my winding journey culminating in the creation of this book.

I must start with my family – my wife Melanie and my children Beker and Liliye, who have patiently listened to my numerous monologues propounding the harms of screen addiction. They have furnished me with encouragement and strength to keep going.

There has been a close group who I need to mention by name as they have been instrumental in this process. My inner circle – Petra Salva OBE, Shabazz Nelson, Kristian Bolton, Richard Bell and Martin Watson have listened to my ideas and endured my stop-start erratic writing sessions. I was constantly telling them "I will finish it next week", only to be saying the same thing months later – my own inner demons and procrastination taking over, as they so often do. However, we eventually made it!

I am grateful to other close friends who have been generous in their support and helped me stay focussed along the way – Tommy Cunliffe, Clive Lewis MP, Brian and Natalie Ford, Sophie Renaude, Steve Payne, Rich D'Amura, Giray Takar, Neil Poole, Abby Takar, Mus Huseyin and Allison McKechnie. I want to thank Türkay Özkan and his team at Holybella in North Finchley,

London for keeping my eyes open by topping me up with caffeine day after day.

My wild squirrel friends – Spotty, Sneaky, Junior, Gandalf, Spock and Number Four – have been invaluable in keeping me peaceful and connected with nature.

A big thank you goes to everyone that I may not have remembered in my hurry to publish this book.

Finally, with love, I want to acknowledge the solid foundations that equipped me for this life – my parents, Cemaliye and Mehmet, and brothers, Hasan and Hakan, with special mention to my incredibly resilient, funny and life-loving grandmother, Nüriye. They have always told me to reach high and persevere, even when the going might be tough: Never give up, create your own *rebellion* and go for it – no one else will do it for you!

"Rebellions are built on hope!" [1]

Jyn Erso

Glossary of Key Terms

Active Listening: a combination of mastering many skills, including reading body language and tone of voice, maintaining your attention, and being aware of and controlling your emotional response.

AI (Artificial Intelligence): technology that enables computers and machines to simulate human learning, comprehension, problem solving, decision-making, creativity and autonomy.

Anchor: a stimulus that creates a response in either you or in another person. When an individual is at the peak of an experience, during an intense, emotional state, and if a specific stimulus is applied, a neurological link is established between the emotional state and the stimulus.

Bad Actor: a person or organization responsible for actions that are harmful, illegal, or morally wrong.

Credits: encompass coins, credits, V-Bucks and any other in-app purchasing capabilities.

Digital Cocaine: a metaphor for the addictive substance derived from screen usage which drives us back for more, like a drug – always searching for the next hit.

Digital Salivation: the sensation initiated upon hearing a notification ding or a buzz from our phones – we mentally salivate in anticipation of the "reward".

Dopamine: most notably involved in helping us feel pleasure as part of the brain's reward system. Gaming, social media, shopping, smelling cookies baking in the oven — all these things can trigger dopamine release, or a "dopamine rush." This feel-good neurotransmitter is also involved in reinforcement. That's why, once we try one of those cookies, we might come back for another one (or two, or three). The darker side of dopamine is the intense feeling of reward people feel which can lead to addiction.

FoMO (Fear of Missing Out): the uneasy and sometimes all-consuming feeling that you're missing out – that your peers are doing, in the know about, or in possession of more or something better than you.

Gamification: a strategy that integrates entertaining and immersive gaming elements into nongame contexts to enhance engagement and motivate certain behaviours. Gamification uses game design and mechanics, such as badges, leaderboards, points and rewards, to encourage active participation and make tasks fun and enjoyable.

Humane Technology: envisioning a world with technology that respects our attention, improves our well-being, and strengthens communities.

In-App Purchasing: buying additional items within the game itself. Purchasing armour, extensions to cars, weaponry, including additional in-house credits to enable greater purchasing capability within the app.

NLP (Neuro-Linguistic Programming): a collection of tools and techniques to help us recognise and change our patterns of behaviour at the conscious and unconscious level. It also provides a powerful set of tools to leverage the transformational effect of language.

Parent-Coach: a parent, guardian, teacher, social worker or other caregiver who has learned to interact in new and creative ways with children, via the introduction of NLP and coaching techniques in the Combat Screen Addiction programme at www.RebelTherapies.com

Prefrontal Cortex: sits at the front of our brain and is crucial in our decision-making, emotional regulation, future planning, problem-solving, self-control, and acting with long-term goals in mind.

Risky Behaviour: also includes the term risky play and is defined as thrilling and exciting forms of play and behaviour that involve risk of physical injury, as well as having an element of uncertainty to it.

School Phobia and School Anxiety: School refusal is often known as school phobia. It can also be called emotionally-based school avoidance (EBSA) or anxiety-related absence. There is an element of fear for children who do not go to school, a feeling that they cannot cope. They might be anxious about schoolwork, exams, bullying, mental health issues, or struggling with relationships with friends or teachers. Some children feel out of step with their classmates: this is especially true of children who are young for their age and see all the others in their groups as older, more confident and more grown up.

Screen Weaning: the process of weaning yourself and your child off screens, like weaning a baby off their milk bottle.

Synaptic Pathways: Important functions of the prefrontal cortex are established during early life, when neurons exhibit enhanced synaptic plasticity and synaptogenesis. This developmental stage drives the organization of cortical connectivity, responsible for establishing behavioural patterns.

Three Things Rule: Rich D'Amura's rule for focusing on three specific items or activities for efficient use of time and effort.

wyd: "what (are) you doing" – an abbreviation used in social media messaging.

Foreword

In the rapidly changing, ever transforming social world of the twenty-first century some major new challenges have arisen for parents and families. With advances in global technology, these new challenges are presenting personal and psychological issues that are appearing frequently in therapy consulting rooms. Perhaps these problems have always been there, and perhaps it has taken these social changes for them to appear so clearly. I cannot know, but children are drawing our attention to their struggles through a range of behavioural communications revealing cries for help.

At the hub of every family is a parental relationship, and how this functions is central to children born into their space. The way in which parents adapt themselves individually and collectively will psychologically impact the child's understanding of themselves and the world they inhabit. When a child is born, every parental relationship will face many difficulties. If the relationship is well-functioning the child is protected from the struggles that arise. This will include interferences caused by the child to the parental relationship.

The mother, always the child's primary relationship, will suffer during pregnancy and profoundly in the following months. How the mother's suffering is supported bears huge significance upon the infant for she will need external help to manage her nurturing role. If the father – or supporting other – is available and able to bear their own needs, they can provide much needed support for the mother. In a well-functioning parental relationship, the child can remain largely unaffected and unaware of the adult strains around them. This can be seen as the psychological foundation for a healthy life.

During the child's early life, the functionality of the parental relationship does not need to be perfect, it just needs to be 'good-enough'. By this I mean the child receives enough benign, kind, and attentive care to feel safe and 'know' that mum is available when needed.

On the flip side are circumstances where the child does not receive enough nurturing care. This may come about if the parental relationship has broken down. Perhaps the father is unable to support himself or the mother, or she has unresolved personal matters that cloud her mind at crucial times etc. In such situations, the child can suffer and develop psychological problems. Children growing up under these circumstances, create different ways to communicate their suffering, and these methods will depend upon their age and other dynamics.

One common form of communication is through behaviour, where children act out their emotions. If these communications are unnoticed, misunderstood or neglected, the child can be perceived as problematic. It is here my theoretical thinking meets reality. It is where Munur and his clients become linked. It is where the child and family unit – who are often unaware of why their child is acting out – need help. It is where this book becomes so important.

Technology has become a major medium for social interaction. Perhaps COVID accelerated this when people – normally available for regular support – became unavailable and accessible largely through computers, phones and tablets etc. Lives changed and new habits were formed. Parents struggling with themselves, their lives, work, and relationships etc., increasingly introduced screens as a supportive parental tool. The child's need for parental attention has not changed. Nor has the primal need for the mother or other supporting adults to provide it. Screens cannot replace it, and where maternal care is significantly reduced, withdrawn or neglected, children are suffering.

This book is a fascinating collection of case studies and insights into a modern-day problem.

Martin Watson, *Psychoanalytic supervisor (SAP) and psychodynamic psychotherapist. BPC accredited and MBACP.*

Introduction

I should be dead.

I survived 9/11. I didn't realise it then, but my life took on an entirely different trajectory after that day.

I celebrate two birthdays a year. One is for the day my mother gave birth to me. The other is for the day when my journey to the World Trade Centre, and a breakfast meeting on the 106th floor in Windows on the World, was diverted.

That horrific day precipitated a monumental shift in my mindset. I went from being money-focused within my investment banking career to wanting to make a difference, but not knowing what that calling meant for me.

I had moved to New York on Saturday 8th September 2001 as I was part of the winning team selected to deliver a technology project to Citigroup. I stayed at the Roosevelt Hotel just next to Grand Central Station in Midtown while I settled into life in New York. My wife, Melanie, remained in London with the intention of joining me within a few months if the project went well.

On the morning of Tuesday 11th September, I had got myself ready, having planned to head down to the Borders bookstore in 5 WTC (World Trade Centre), to then go to a breakfast meeting at Windows on the World. Fortunately, I never made it there and neither did my colleague, Peter, who had been waiting in the Wall Street office for my confirmation call that didn't come.

In getting ready for my first day on the project with Citigroup, I grabbed a coffee and pastry in the hotel's restaurant, having left my suit jacket and laptop on the bed in my room. Normally I have everything with me but on this occasion I did something out of character.

I got back to my tiny room, intending to grab my laptop bag and suit jacket, spin round and leave again, before the door could close. But before that could happen, all within 5-10 seconds, the hotel phone rang. I was in two minds whether to take the call as I had to get down to the WTC to meet Peter. I answered the phone. It was Melanie calling to wish me good luck for my first day. But what was meant to be a brief two minute call turned into something much longer.

Melanie began the conversation lightly but became emotionally overwhelmed, which was also out of character, especially since she was at work. She said that she missed me more than she expected and decided to drop everything to come over to New York as soon as she could organise it. In that moment, my concern was for my wife, and so we spent the next 50 minutes on the call.

As the call took so long, I missed the opportunity to head downtown to the WTC to meet Peter and decided that it would be better to go directly to Citigroup Tower in Queens instead. I called Peter, who agreed to meet me there later that morning. I left my hotel close to 8:45am, made it to the 7 train and over to LIC (Long Island City) in Queens.

My life changed in an instant when the train pulled out of the tunnel in Queens. People started screaming, pointing out of the window towards downtown Manhattan. The 1 WTC had smoke bellowing from the top part of the building. What came next is something I will never forget. I saw the second plane fly into the second WTC tower. From that moment, I remember everything in slow motion.

My feelings around being a survivor have always been fraught with difficulty. Sadness and happiness have coexisted, and this conflict has driven me forward with a purpose that has taken time to realise.

I've had many ups and some noticeably big downs since that terrible day, trying to understand my role on this beautiful planet. I have spent a lot of time working out who I want to be as a person, a husband, father, brother, son, and friend. This has led to the path I am on now. I want to make a positive impact on the world in the best way I can.

Today, as a 23-year-old living in a 53-year-old body, I recognise I have been given a second chance, a chance to do some good and give back in a way that I hadn't really understood prior to 9/11.

Wake Up

This journey has culminated in me "waking up" to the complex systems so effectively used by the powerful tech giants to manipulate the unsuspecting general population.

In starting my mission seven years ago, my research uncovered the subtle behavioural changes that were being massaged into our delicate brains by the technology delivered through our smartphones, tablets and similar devices. By learning about the techniques which capture and sell our attention to the highest bidders, and becoming fully aware of their detrimental effects, I have been able to understand the various players involved in my own screen addiction, experiment with different techniques on myself and alter my own behaviour. My "wake up" to tech has given me greater freedom, enabling me to regain control of my life, thus allowing me to spend my time as I see fit.

During my normal day-to-day I see so many people being sucked in by their devices, acting like digital zombies. Parents stick devices in front of their young children, oblivious to the potential long-term harm it is doing. Daily I see countless people ignoring each other as they stare into their devices, people meeting in cafés, and once seated, being more engrossed in their phones than the company they are with.

- What is so important that they need to continuously check their phones at the expense of the people they are with?
- Is it because their present company is not as interesting as the content on their device?

When I get on the tube to travel into central London, I see more of the same. People that once took time to read a book or newspaper now stare down at their little pocket rocket computer, absorbing continuous dopamine[1] hits into their brains, blissfully unaware of their surroundings, barely looking up to see what is happening around them.

Case Studies

The case studies in this book have been compiled from my session notes with clients over the past several years. I have tried to give you an idea of how things unfolded in each case and how we worked together to look forward in a positive way, taking uncomfortable action at times to enable change to occur at the very deepest of levels – change that would be long-lasting, not just quick fixes.

The names, locations, and some private details of my clients have been changed to protect their identities. I believe these stories are a valuable platform for learning and understanding, a reference point for many others in similar situations to help them make positive change in their lives.

This book has been created to allow you, the reader, to read just one chapter, a few chapters, or all chapters in whichever order suits you. The case studies are independent of each other, and each one shows the different ways I have been able to help the parents and their children to make the necessary changes in their lives to reconnect with family and friends, and rethink their future relationship with technology.

This is not a technology-bashing book, it is a book highlighting the importance of connection, specifically within families, and how we can reignite the way we interact with each other. It is about rescuing and preventing our children from entering an abyss that is not yet fully understood and helping them in a considered and compassionate way as they adjust to this new world. It is about giving our children the very best platform to safely navigate through the unregulated dense jungle that is the online world.

Having gone through this very journey myself as an addict, forever connected to my Blackberry and then iPhone, I was consumed by the behavioural change drivers that were pulling me into the rabbit-hole of the online world to the detriment of my relationships with family and friends. Waking up and seeing what was happening to me and my children, who were equally addicted to their social media and gaming, I decided to act.

I wanted to help others become self-aware, to notice what was happening and to help reduce the effects of screen harm and addiction and, even more so, to have families reconnect, to help them reclaim their relationships. So, I created a programme based on the strategies and techniques I learnt along the way. These were tried and tested on myself and my family and then on others wanting similar change.

I hope to bring these strategies and techniques to life in these case studies, and if all I do here is raise your awareness to make some positive change in your life with your family and friends, and help change the way you interact with your tech, then hopefully I will have made a difference.

These case studies illustrate difficult and sometimes scary situations parents have found themselves in, which have required immediate intervention. My intention is to be able to help parents in a preventative way and highlight what might be happening in their family units so that they can pull the right levers to course correct and take action to create a positive outcome for both themselves and their children.

To get the very best out of this book, please feel free to use the blank pages at the end of the book to make notes of your thoughts and feelings and write down any questions you may have. You will also find a QR code at the end of each chapter directing you to our Rebel Insights information page, if you would like to download or print any of the tips and techniques suggested.

Chapter 1

How Young Is Too Young?

My Combat Screen Addiction coaching was sparked off in 2018 when I was coaching Fiona, who had been a client of mine for three months. We had been focusing specifically on personal performance coaching and how she could take her business "to the next level".

Fiona, a successful businesswoman, was running her own small legal firm in London at the time. She had focused on her career in the first part of her adult life, working tirelessly to make a name for herself in the City, in a male-dominated legal world. Having set up her business as her first priority in 2005, she turned her attention to marrying her long-term boyfriend in 2010.

Whenever Fiona put her mind to something, she would master it, whether that was excelling in her legal exams, or running 10k in record time at her local running club. But despite her success, Fiona had an overwhelming feeling that she must constantly prove herself. Most of the time, underneath that confident and strong outward-facing persona, she felt like an imposter, worried that she would be "found out". The success would always come with the sense of not quite feeling safe, fitting in, or being "adequate" – a word she used a great deal in our sessions.

Fiona began our session by telling me that she didn't have the energy to even speak, let alone complete the session. This was quite out of character as she'd usually dive energetically into our sessions with focus and passion. This was the first time I learnt about the problems Fiona and her husband Paul were having with their daughter, Sarah, and her astonishing dependency on screens.

Fiona had been struggling to negotiate with Sarah over screen use, and this was causing a great deal of angst because previously she had not set any limits on her daughter's engagement with digital devices.

Fiona broke down. Sobbing uncontrollably, she called herself a "failure" as a mother and a wife, saying she was worried sick about the turn her home life had taken. Fiona explained that her daughter's intense device addiction was causing a dangerous rift in her marriage, mainly because she couldn't see eye to eye with Paul on how to deal with "Sarah's addiction".

It is particularly tough when one parent is willing to allow a smartphone or digital device, and the other parent has an opposing view. Fiona explained that it was her own fault initially; she would allow Sarah to use the smartphone whereas Paul was dead against it, saying that it would cause them problems in the long term.

Their difference of opinion over their daughter's phone use generated lingering tension between Fiona and Paul and they argued frequently.

As Fiona divulged all this, she asked me to do whatever I could to help her and her family. She asked two clear things of me in that session:

- Help me find a way to stop my daughter's screen addiction.
- Help me save my marriage!

I was saddened to find out that Fiona and Paul were in this situation, especially when she told me their daughter was only 18 months old!

Here were two parents struggling to agree about how much screen time to give to their toddler. The situation should never have arisen – it's a problem created by using screens as a parent substitute. They allowed their daughter to fall into a trap of digital desires.

Is infant usage of phones becoming far too common? When I step outside, walk down the high street into a café, I look around and I see this all too regularly, and it's not just in the UK. Parents are unwittingly setting their children up for a range of developmental issues as well as creating long-term addictive habits, perhaps because of lackadaisical attitudes within our current society but also a lack of well targeted educational support.

What surprised me was seeing two educated, professional and successful adults willing to give their child screens to gain some peace and quiet. To quote Fiona, "my days are so busy, I just need some quiet time when it comes to breakfast or dinner. I need to just have my child eat her food without needing me because that's the only time I have for me."

During what I call our crossover session from performance coaching to Combat Screen Addiction coaching, Fiona listed her main concerns about her daughter's screen use. Fiona told me that Sarah would demand the phone the moment she woke up in the morning, and not relinquish it until she went to bed at night. She wouldn't fall asleep unless she had the phone next to her, with the phone light switched on. If she woke up in the middle of the night she would scream because by then Fiona would have taken her phone back and the room would be pitch black. If Sarah couldn't feel the phone beside her then she would throw a tantrum.

It was an incredibly stressful time in their lives, as they had just moved into a new home, hired a new nanny, and Fiona was actively trying to get back into working full-time in her business. There were lots of teething problems as they adjusted to their new home and circumstances.

Fiona listed all the scenarios in which Sarah presented her digital device demands:

- Sarah would demand the phone while she was sitting in her highchair having breakfast.
- Sarah would only take a bath if she had a screen beside the bath playing a children's show.
- Sarah would only get into the car if they had the iPad with them.
- Sarah would only eat her lunch with a screen in front of her.
- Sarah would only eat dinner with the screen in front of her.
- Sarah would only sit quietly in a coffee shop or a restaurant if there was a screen in front of her.
- Sarah didn't want to play with the new nanny as she preferred to watch a screen.

Fiona explained that it was a nightmare to walk into Sarah's room in the middle of the night. Fiona or Paul would only go into the room if they heard Sarah crying for attention. To placate her, they walked into her room with the phone light switched on. This would make Sarah aware of the phone and then she would be on a mission to take it from her parents.

When I asked Fiona why they continued to enter Sarah's room with the smartphone light on, she had no real response apart from "well it's the only thing that we could do". Fiona and Paul were so stuck in a rut that they couldn't think of anything else they could do to stop Sarah's unyielding behaviour towards digital devices.

Working on this problem was a priority for us, and it was a problem I had a very easy solution for. However, looking from the outside it sometimes seems as if the solution to a problem is easy and obvious; when someone is overwhelmed with stress and anxiety, they are often unable to see beyond their nose.

Good coaching is not about telling your client what the solution is – it's about helping them understand where they're at and what they themselves can do to solve their problem. They need to tap into their own internal resources and capability to think clearly. If they take time to reflect, they will eventually become more aware of the wider context of their situation and be able to generate an effective solution independently.

Sarah's Digital Device Demands

Fiona told me many stories about Sarah's behaviour and how the use of smartphones and devices dominated her life.

When Sarah woke up each morning she would search her bed for the phone. If it wasn't there, she would scream until one of her parents brought a phone to her. This placated her for a while but did more harm than good, because giving in to Sarah just caused Fiona and Paul more and more stress. The stress was exacerbated by the couple arguing about whose turn it was that morning to give up their phone. It habituated behaviour which was destructive and facilitated Sarah's complete reliance on digital devices.

It also reinforced a process by which Sarah was able to control the behaviour of her parents and the nanny. It taught Sarah to use distress and "unbearable" noise to overcome any obstacles to getting her own way.

The angst this caused Fiona and Paul threatened to destroy their marriage. Their relationship nosedived around the same time they introduced devices into Sarah's life. They had hugely different opinions on when and why to give a device to Sarah. Paul didn't really want Sarah to use devices at all but did not argue his case strongly enough to Fiona. Fiona told me that she had no real opinion at the beginning as she didn't really understand the problems it would cause. Fiona likened device usage to the days of watching TV when she was a child. She thought letting Sarah sit with an iPad on her lap was the same as Sarah sitting in front of the TV.

Truth is, the difference is startling. Screen-life even 20 years ago bears absolutely no relation to screen-life since the introduction of tablets and smartphones.

What is now clear to Fiona is that the TV is stationary, often watched as a family and can be switched off easily with minimal pushback and aggression. However, the iPad or smartphone is entirely different because it's fully mobile. Sarah was able to take it everywhere with her. At the touch of a button and swipe on a screen, Sarah could entertain herself with the entire internet readily available. She could be exposed to anything and everything because there were no filters on the devices she had access to.

After our conversations where she came to understand the full impact that screens were having on Sarah, Fiona now realises the adverse behavioural change in Sarah that she allowed to happen by not having a strict policy on screen time.

This is a disturbing issue, and one that poses great risk to our young children. Many parents I have worked with don't know about, or bother to activate, parenting restrictions on these devices. I have dealt with many parents and grandparents who don't have much experience with technology.

In Fiona's case, she knew about child restrictions but didn't bother with them as Sarah was too young and could not possibly be viewing inappropriate sites.

Paul was a tech-savvy guy and knew about restrictions, but he didn't bother with the restrictions either, because he'd have to set them up on his own smartphone and iPad, and that would be too frustrating for him.

Knowing about these restrictions and not applying them is problematic. I challenged both Paul and Fiona about this during our sessions because it was crucial for their understanding and self-awareness, and essential to move forward and attempt to change their lives in a positive way.

Car Troubles Anyone?

Another challenge for Fiona was the inability to get Sarah into the car for any journey, long or short, without a screen playing *Peppa Pig* on repeat. This caused some of the most brutal disagreements between Fiona and Paul. They had huge arguments while getting Sarah in the car, so that all three of them would be upset before the journey had even started. Any trip the family took was preceded by three painful steps.

Step 1 – Tantrum

It would always start off with Sarah throwing a tantrum unless the iPad was strapped to the headrest in front of her. Once the iPad was in place, the sound was turned up so high that it was often hard for the driver to focus on driving. If there were interruptions to the smooth running of her programme, Sarah would scream uncontrollably – startling the driver, which almost caused several crashes.

Step 2 – Fireworks for Fiona and Paul

Sarah's tantrums would always lead to Fiona and Paul arguing about why they had to go through this pain every time they were in the car with their daughter. They would accuse one another of causing the tantrums by not having the iPad set up and ready for Sarah before she got to the car. Paul would often blame Fiona for the whole situation, telling her they shouldn't have to do this every time and that they should just "let her cry until she passes out". This was an empty threat, however, and before my intervention the couple hadn't really tried to stop Sarah's antics in the car. Even the nanny, Sally, would be drawn into this and be blamed for not having everything ready for Sarah's fraught entry into the car.

I met with Sally separately as I had to get a third person's view on what was going on in the household.

When I met Sally, she was at her wit's end and threatening to quit. She told me that every day of the three months she had worked there had been a nightmare and the main cause of all the problems in the household was Sarah's screen usage.

Sally told me the inaction of Fiona and Paul and their incapability to put in place "some simple boundaries" and agree a way to manage Sarah's screen usage was their downfall and would "most probably be the end to their marriage". Sally was completely opposed to Sarah's screen use and would often be told off by Fiona and Paul if she tried mentioning weaning Sarah off screens. Sally painted a very clear picture of the family unit which corroborated Fiona's account and gave me greater insight into their relationships.

Step 3 – Angry Drive

After settling Sarah into the comfort of her screen, with the crying, screaming, shouting, and blame-throwing calmed, they would be able to start their journey. The journey was always tense, with an angry atmosphere in the car. The trip would generally be without conversation, while *Peppa Pig* broadcast repeatedly, with the occasional shrieks of Sarah's laughter, or her screams of frustration if there were any interruptions to her screen use.

Fiona explained that they would always get to their destination feeling tense and frustrated, apart from Sarah who would be happy with the screentime viewing. Even when they reached their destination the screen would be part of the outing, whether it was seeing friends, shopping, or going somewhere to eat. There was no downtime of digital devices. It was also essential that they had a portable charger with them at all times, and it had to be fully charged. Sarah's wrath was too overbearing to deal with if a device "ran out of juice".

This situation was untenable, and Paul and Fiona's marriage was near breaking point. The strain they were under had already prompted a move into separate bedrooms, something I did not find out about in the first three months of coaching Fiona before she told me about Sarah's screen addiction.

It didn't help that nearly every conversation Paul and Fiona had ended up with them discussing Sarah's screen addiction and saying horrible things to each other in blame-filled anger. I relate these painful details of the family's situation to show what can happen to relationships, and to people's emotional, physical and mental wellbeing if there is inaction as a consequence of a lack of understanding of the issues they face.

In this case the unhelpful combination of inaction and lack of understanding allowed Sarah to rule the household by demanding unfettered access to devices. Sarah's screen use became so bad that she would also demand a screen of any type when she was getting ready for a bath, while in the bath and when getting out of the bath. A screen had to be available nearly every waking hour otherwise the wrath of Sarah would be unleashed. At times Fiona or Paul would give Sarah a device before she "kicked off", to prevent the arguments they invariably had when she was "misbehaving". It became a tool to keep the peace between her parents.

Sarah wouldn't eat, sleep, bath or get in the car without a screen in tow. Fiona and Paul were being controlled by the tantrums of an 18-month-old, who was only behaving according to the environment that was created for her.

I have come across this many times in the past few years and I continually find myself bewildered about where the parents disappeared to in the build-up to these desperately sad situations. It feels as if it's easier to turn a blind eye, for whatever reason, to what is happening around them because they don't want to deal with the situation.

Some of these parents have told me that they have "too much going on", or they were unaware of what was unfolding, or that they lost touch with their child … and it is not their fault. Invariably they tell me that they thought if they let things play out the situation would get better with time, and their child would get bored of social media, or gaming, or YouTube, or pornography. Needless to say, things don't usually turn out that way.

This is because of the addictive pull of the devices and the digital cocaine-filled technology that they have in their homes. Free will is ripped from you. The control of your brain and eyeballs belongs to the apps, constantly emitting a "ding" or a flashing notification to train you to pick up the device, just like Pavlov's dog and the bell – what I call "digital salivation".

For those who haven't come across the reference, Pavlov illustrated that by using the sound of a bell, dogs could be conditioned to salivate if that sound was repeatedly presented while they were given food. By taking the dogs through this conditioning Pavlov found that even when there was no food present and he rang the bell, the dogs would salivate. This is no different to our conditioning with smartphones and digital devices. The "ding" (bell) has us salivating at what might be lying in wait. Even when there is no bell, the mere thought of a smartphone triggers a desire to check what we have received.

It became clear from my discussions with Fiona and Paul that they had become lost. It was never their intention to let things get as bad as they did for Sarah, or for their relationship to flounder. It was only through sheer luck that Fiona managed to find the one business coach that specialised in combating screen addition for parents and their children.

The Strategy – Sarah's Digital Detox

In each of my case studies, I find it's important to understand as much as possible about the family, extended family and their friends to understand how their relationships work, where the problem points are, the barriers, the positive influences and supporters of change and the negative influences, which I use to create a strategy tailor-made for the specific case.

Stage 1 – Screen Weaning

Our very first action was to change Sarah's relationship with screens so that we could eventually remove screens completely from her life. As Sarah was so young, her brain was changing and learning so quickly that it was a fast process to remove the screens and for her to forget they ever existed. We were able to divert Sarah's attention at each main stress point where devices were involved, effectively implementing a complete digital detox.

This started with a very simple but very effective change to Sarah's routine at bedtime and through the night. We introduced a penguin night light that could double up as a little portable torch.

Fiona and Paul introduced the penguin when Sarah was having one of her tantrums in the middle of the night. Fiona walked in with the penguin light on, and Sarah immediately stopped her tantrum. She was so mesmerised by the penguin she didn't mention the phone with its light.

There was a near-immediate change that almost knocked Fiona and Paul off their feet. Sarah took to the penguin and the portable light in the penguin's belly immediately. Fiona told me she spent the next two hours in her own bedroom shaking and crying; she couldn't believe the impact of something so simple. Sarah no longer asked for the phone light as it was probably not as interesting or as much fun as the penguin light. This became the new normal.

Sometimes it's the simplest things in life that have the most profound and unexpected positive effect on us. The penguin certainly had that effect in this situation.

The second and slightly harder part of the screen weaning process was removing the devices from Sarah during the day. It took about 10 days in total to remove and replace them with other things to fill the void of the screen. It started with mealtimes. Instead of the smartphone or the tablet, we caught her attention with music and a couple of toy cars which she had enjoyed playing with in the time before screens had been introduced to her.

To support the early stages of this changeover, Fiona and Paul gave Sarah an old second-hand smartphone at mealtimes. It had no battery life and therefore nothing was displayed on the screen. It was so effective that by the third mealtime, Sarah had lost all interested in the phone and started playing with her cars and grooving in her highchair to the music her parents were playing to her.

Picture 1. Illustration of Sarah's Penguin and Portable Light

I suggested introducing the Australian version of *Hi-5*, a children's TV show that educates and entertains through play, movement and music, and is a lot of fun. The programme was a delightful resource for my children and others we have introduced it to during the last 15-20 years. Fiona and Paul bought the CDs of the programme then played them and sang to Sarah while she ate. The transformative nature of these two interventions at bedtime and mealtimes was miraculous and changed the entire mood of the house.

Sally commented on the change within just two weeks of our intervention. She said that not only had I saved little Sarah from the oblivion of zombie screen life, but there was also a thawing in Fiona and Paul's relationship. Sally also told me this new normal had completely changed her mind about her job, and she was considering staying.

We progressed to bathtime and car journeys. The toy cars enjoyed during mealtimes were also introduced at bathtime and were a hit. Car journeys were transformed by playing music and singing songs together. Fiona and Paul also introduced visual games like naming the colours of the passing cars or "looking for doggies". The change-around was a breath of fresh air.

Stage 2 – Relationship Fix 101

Repairing the relationship between all parties, especially that of Fiona and Paul, was paramount in keeping this family together and creating a future with the highest positive intentions for them in mind.

I worked with Fiona and Paul to make a list of activities they were prepared to try with their renewed energy and commitment. We then drew up a detailed day-to-day diary including these new activities, which would give them quality time to repair their fractious marriage.

This included a specific timeslot to sit and reflect on each other's day, without any discussion of Sarah. Before their daughter was born, they had enjoyed doing this regularly. They had been each other's support, and this had suffered immeasurably since Sarah's birth, especially during the 3-6 months before they had engaged with me.

We added date nights and some fantastic family days out which involved nature-only days, and weekends away both with and without Sarah. It was essential for them to find that time, energy and closeness to rekindle their love.

We also discussed the elephant in the room, which was their parenting strategy, and unpacked this in a safe and considerate way, adopting clearly agreed parameters for active listening.[1] This process was very effective in helping Fiona and Paul understand their situation more clearly and reframe the events with a positive forward-thinking mindset.

Stage 3 – The Journey

The icing on the cake was the third stage of this strategy, which was done simultaneously with Sarah's weaning off devices. Everything we had introduced needed to be cemented into the very fabric of the family's everyday lives as second nature.

This took quite a bit of getting used to for Fiona and Paul as it meant making sure they kept their smartphones and tablets completely out of sight. If they needed to use those devices, they had to do so in a space where Sarah wouldn't be able to see them.

It meant that they had to adopt some key time management skills, and a change of mindset for themselves, as well as getting others to understand that they wouldn't be responding to their messages or emails immediately. They bought a landline, which meant that if anyone needed them urgently while they were at home they could be contacted via the home phone. They soon found that they very rarely received a call on their home phone as nothing was really that urgent.

Conclusion

Six Months On

In those first three months when I worked with Fiona on Sarah's screen addiction, I introduced different ideas, strategies, tools and techniques that she could use with Sarah to carefully remove smartphones and any other devices with a screen. I introduced a strategy for Fiona and Paul to understand and repair their relationship and manage their own screen usage.

Fiona later told me they had been the best three months of her adult life. Her relationship with Paul was firmly back on track, and the relationship with Sarah was everything she had wished for. Fiona said the best way to explain how she felt was that she had switched out of a horror film and was now living in a happy Disney fairytale where the Princess meets her Prince and they live happily ever after. This is not to say that there would not be any future ups and downs, frustrations, and disagreements, but for now she was "walking on air".

Fiona and Paul took on all the advice, techniques and strategies, as they changed so many small things in their lives. Instead of bowing down to all of Sarah's protests and demands, they removed technology from her eyeline, and replaced it with interaction, engagement, life, energy and joy. Focusing their energy in a positive way towards their daughter completely transformed their lives.

The tech devices did not exist for Sarah anymore! The tantrums that 18-month-old Sarah had whenever she saw the smartphone or tablet had become a thing of the past. It was an incredible turnaround.

Six Years On

I recently caught up with Fiona during our quarterly family check-up, and things were still going well. They had religiously kept technological devices away and would hold off from introducing these devices to Sarah, now 8, and her 2-year-old sister, Bella. Fiona mentioned that they now had a wonderful family togetherness and that "Sarah plays beautifully with Bella".

Sarah was kept away from screens and all her friends' parents had been gently asked to keep screens away whenever she had a play date with any of her friends. In fact, Fiona advised some of those parents about what she went through back in 2018, and now some of her friends had incorporated the very same strategies and techniques into their own lives.

Fiona and Paul were now immensely proud of their parenting approach to screens and sometimes "showed off" about their baptism of fire with Sarah, and how they navigated through the pain to where they were now. Fiona boasted that Bella was yet to see or understand what a smartphone looked like. She was happily playing with toys and flipping through books, chewing whatever she could as she went through her teething process. It was wonderful to see the progression in their family and to be a positive and ongoing part of their journey.

This point is worth emphasising. Parenting is an ongoing journey and things will continually change. We must learn to adapt and change with it – as our children grow, so do we. It doesn't matter if a child is 18 months old or 18 years old, we still have to look after them – help and guide them. That is part of our journey as parent-coaches. We need to ensure we are good role models, showing our children what "good" looks like. To do this, we need to consider our own relationship with technology and consciously change how we use our devices. Until we do that for ourselves and do it effectively with purpose, passion and energy we won't be able to do this for our children.

The beauty of this case study is that it shows that change can happen, and it can happen quickly. This is an ongoing process … it doesn't stop. It doesn't stop today, and it certainly does not stop tomorrow. Ongoing commitment to these strategies and techniques will help to reclaim, reinforce, and enhance your relationship with your children, partner, extended family and friends.

If you would like to know more about becoming a parent-coach, scan the QR code below for the Rebel Insights page at www.RebelTherapies.com where you can find various downloadable information sheets and top tips which are mentioned in this book.

Chapter 2

The Nude Predator!

The online world is full of bad actors[1] – individuals and groups who create pain and harm in various ways. Gangs live off crime through extortion and blackmail, hidden behind what usually looks like carefree and gentle personas. In this case study we explore how a bad actor enticed a vulnerable teenager through carefully controlled contact, creating trust and abusing that trust to blackmail and extort, causing untold stress, anxiety, pain and depression.

Help My Son

I remember when I received the call for help from Mike late one evening. He just said:

> *"I have a real problem with my son. He's going to do something really bad. Someone we both know said you could help. Can you? Will you?"*

I immediately asked Mike if his son was at risk of taking his own life. If that was the case, I would refer him to emergency resources such as the Samaritans, Mind and Childline. Mike was unsure! We agreed to have a Zoom call to determine whether emergency action was required or if Ben was in a good enough space to work with me.

During our face-to-face meeting on Zoom, Mike gave me the background to the utter devastation that had engulfed his family.

He explained that this call was a culmination of six weeks of investigative work. He had noticed some changes in his son, Ben, who was 16 at the time. Normally a very cheerful chap, always joking with his 10-year-old sister, Ben was pretty much the light of the family when he was around.

When Ben came back from Sixth Form, he would usually spend time having a debrief with his mum – a general catch-up on what had happened that day and how his schoolwork was going.

Mike became aware that Ben started spending more time in his room than with the family. He became very secretive, whereas before he was usually quite open about what was going on.

Mike was sure that something was up and during the first call I needed to find out all the facts before we could put together a strategy. We brainstormed all the things that Ben usually did when he was "normal". These were:

- Fully involved in family life when he returned home from Sixth Form each day
- Playing games with his sister as often as he possibly could
- Talking with his mum
- Lightness
- Positive mindset
- Happy mood most of the time
- Spending time watching sports and movies with his dad
- Looking alive
- Taking care with his appearance
- Washing daily
- Eating well

- Having regular sleeping patterns
- Regular attendance at Sixth Form
- Taking care with his homework and handing in on time
- A good network of friends who he met in person and caught up with when playing games online
- Working out at the gym and at home – physically very fit

These behaviours didn't all change in one go. The changes happened little by little. Over a relatively short period, Ben's personality shifted from happy and easy-going to secretive and closed off from his family.

Ben steadily declined into what his parents refer to as "shrivelled up Ben".

Mike initially thought that Ben's behaviour had only changed in relation to his family. However, over the course of the next few weeks he received messages from Ben's friendship group as well as a couple of calls from his school.

Ben's friends had also noticed a distinct change in his personality and were concerned for him. When they broached this subject with Ben, he told his friends nothing was wrong and that he was just not feeling too great; he practically disappeared from all the group chats and gaming sessions. It was odd because he had been the centre of the group and the main driver of the online group sessions.

Learning from Ben's friends that he was just as withdrawn with them as he was at home sparked numerous confrontations at home between Mike and Ben. When Mike was at work, Andrea (Ben's mum) would try interacting with Ben. This would always end badly, with Ben screaming and shouting at his mum. He would constantly tell his parents to "mind their own business" and that they were invading his personal space.

There would be times when Ben lost his temper and flew off the handle, often screaming at his parents. This was very unlike the "normal Ben" … the new Ben was the opposite of the kind, loving, easy-going person that his family knew.

The catalyst for Mike's call to me came one afternoon when Ben returned from Sixth Form. Ben was approached by Andrea in the kitchen during one of their rare sightings of him as he was getting a drink. Within moments things escalated, and Ben flew out of control, so much so that he threatened his mother and pushed her hard against the kitchen cabinets. This was the very first time he had used his physicality towards his mum. Andrea was terrified by this as Ben was much bigger and stronger than she was. She saw a completely different side to her son – certainly not the gentle young man she had raised.

Andrea conveyed the story directly to Mike when he arrived home that evening after a long day at work. This was the tipping point. The fact that Ben had used physical force towards his mum sent Mike into a rage. Mike explained that he burst into Ben's room "absolutely seeing red". He was ready for a physical confrontation with his son. However, what happened next completely shocked him. Instead of Ben reacting as aggressively as Mike, "he just shrivelled up in a ball on his bed and started uncontrollably sobbing".

It took about an hour for all of them to calm down and to finally learn the truth behind Ben's behaviour and what had happened to turn this boy into a shadow of himself.

Beautiful Blackmail

Ben spent the next couple of hours describing in detail what he had been going through in the past few months. He told Mike that he had met a girl online, she'd become involved in all his social groups, enticed him, gained his trust, and then blackmailed him. I have broken down how Ben's situation unfolded into six stages:

Stage 1 – Initial Contact

The girl in question was Emma, a 16-year-old. She told Ben she lived in Windsor, which wasn't too far away. Emma had initially sent Ben an invitation to connect with her. Ben didn't normally accept and connect with someone he didn't already know. However, in this case he made an exception. There were two reasons for this:

1. Emma was already connected to a few of his close friends in his network, and…
2. Emma was very pretty.

Both facts meant Emma got the green light and Ben accepted her invitation to connect.

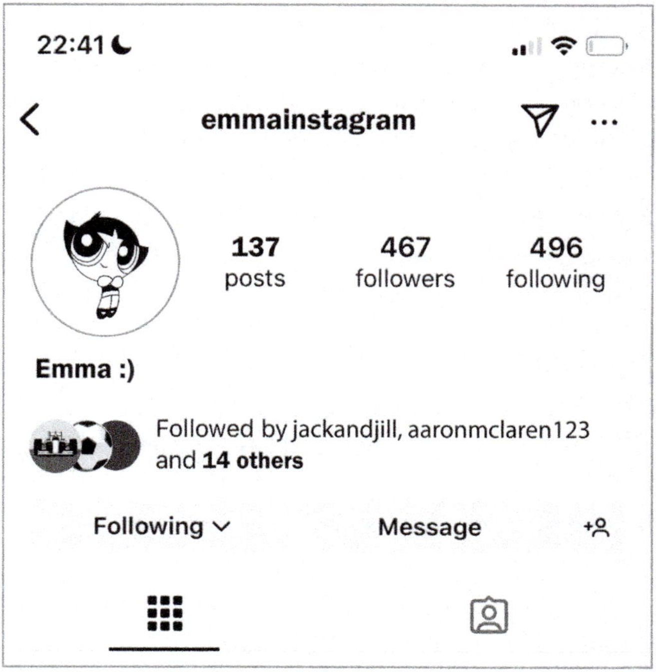

Picture 1. Emma's Instagram

Ben's acceptance of the invitation unwittingly opened the door for the most brutal of manipulations. Emma started messaging almost immediately. Initially the messages were small talk, about what hobbies they liked doing, their favourite bands/singers/music, and where they liked to go in London.

The messages became flirtier as time went on. Emma "confessed" that she felt a greater "connection" with Ben than others in their group of online friends. She also mentioned that the other boys were not as mature, funny, insightful, or as interesting as Ben. She confessed that she'd "checked out" Ben's Instagram profile and liked the fact that he looked after himself and was "pretty fit". Ben, like many teenage boys, was constantly posting photos of his biceps on Instagram after a workout.

Stage 2 – Photo Exchange

The next stage was the photo exchange. This started gradually with Emma sending Ben a blurry picture of herself sitting at her desk in her bedroom. At first the pictures they exchanged were basic and mundane, the ones of Emma usually blurry and those of Ben usually clear. Emma blamed her old phone and camera for the out-of-focus shots, and said her parents would be giving her a much better smartphone for her next birthday, which she mentioned was a few weeks away.

Emma became an active member of their online groups and would generally post something every day in the chat, and everything seemed normal. Ben had no reason to suspect that Emma was not all that she seemed.

But then Ben and Emma's personal conversations started to get even more flirtatious. Emma made Ben promise not to share any of her photos or messages with his friends; she wanted to keep their growing relationship completely confidential.

What Ben didn't know was that Emma was doing exactly the same thing with a couple of his close friends. Emma was clearly in the driving seat in these exchanges, moving them in the direction she wanted to. For Emma, controlling Ben was like having a puppy dog in tow. He would do whatever she wanted, giving her unconditional attention as she teased him, giving Ben a treat every now and then to keep him keen and loyal.

All the boys that she was in "conversations" with were so excited by the fact that Emma was interested in them that they threw out all reasoning and gave in to nearly all her demands. I say "nearly all" her demands, because as her demands for more explicit messages, pictures and then videos ramped up, some of the boys decided it was too much and stopped playing Emma's dangerous game.

Ben, however, felt so privileged that Emma was showing such an interest in him that he gave in each time she asked for more – whether that was a written or voice message, picture or video. This was his downfall. Ben continued to keep the relationship very private.

As Emma's personal messages to Ben became more explicit, she started sending Ben photos of herself in different poses. This escalated into sending pictures with just her underwear on. What Ben didn't pick up on was that nearly all these photos obscured Emma's face, and when her face was fully shown, it was often very blurry. This didn't matter to Ben; he was just delighted that "Gorgeous Emma" was paying attention to him.

Ben reciprocated in the photo trading with Emma. He started taking more photos of himself wearing fewer clothes, eventually ending up sending many photos of him in just his boxer shorts. The messaging continued to get more explicit.

Emma upped the ante and told Ben that she was going to film a video of her stripping to some music, telling him that this is what she would do when they met up in person at his house soon. This tipped Ben over the edge of reason and rational thinking as his testosterone overwhelmed his common sense. He had no capacity to consider the consequences of the actions he was about to take.

Emma then sent him a video of herself stripping to music; however, he could barely make out her face in the video. Later, when I discussed this with Mike, Andrea and Ben, they realised that the video had been filmed in a different location from Emma's other videos, and very likely she was a different girl. This was not something that Ben had noticed or cared about. He was just overjoyed that he had this model-looking "girlfriend", even though they had never met, sending him X-rated videos of herself. He told me that it made him feel "special" that she would do this for him, because she seemed like such an amazing person.

When discussing this with Ben I recognised that this exchange became more one-sided as the messages, pictures and videos became more explicit. Emma's voice also started to change slightly in some of the messages, and her excuse was she had a cold or allergy. For every picture and video that Emma sent, she would demand at least two or three more from Ben, stipulating that they showed his face, and were in focus. Ben spent even more time in his room creating the shots he needed to send to Emma, otherwise she would stop sending him messages.

There were so many opportunities for Ben to become suspicious of Emma and the developing situation, but Ben was oblivious … until the crucial point of this video exchange.

Emma's last video to Ben was supposedly one of her (it clearly was another person) performing a sex act on herself. Off the back of this she demanded multiple nude pictures and videos of Ben, which had to show his private parts. Even though Ben felt some hesitation in doing this, she insisted. She said that if he didn't do what she asked she would walk away, and if he refused, she was sure one of his friends would certainly be "up for it". Ben reluctantly sent a video just as Emma asked.

Emma told him she loved the video, and that it made her feel "excited" and "so happy" that he shared it with her. This made Ben feel good about sending the video. Emma used all her skills to entice Ben to send more videos, including one of him performing a sex act on himself.

This was the turning point and exactly what Emma needed to step up the next part of her vicious scheme.

Stage 3 – Money, Money, Money!

The moment Ben sent the video of himself performing the sex act, Emma had the squeeze on him and Ben's real problems began.

There was a sudden change in Emma's messaging. She told Ben that he had to set up an account on the social media platform, Telegram. Once there, he would be invited to join a group and would be told what to do next.

Emma explained that if he didn't follow her instructions to the letter, she would post his videos and photos to all his friends and groups that she had infiltrated.

Ben initially thought it was a joke – that Emma was just fooling around with him. Surely, she wouldn't do something like that! Unfortunately, Ben could not have been more wrong, and he soon realised this from the new tone of Emma's messages. Her communication became more aggressive, and she failed to answer the frantic messages he sent her in response.

To keep the videos and pictures out of sight of his friendship group and the entire online world, he naively told Emma he would do as she wanted.

Ben created a Telegram account and joined the group as instructed. He was then sent an ultimatum to pay £250 into a specific account within 30 minutes. If he did what she said, she would not release any of the content she had. However, if he didn't comply, the videos would be uploaded to her channel, which had 500,000 subscribers, and she would send his home details to all of them. Emma told him there were some very nasty people in that group and they would want "a piece of him", which would be life-threatening for Ben.

Ben paid the amount immediately and then asked if she would delete all the videos, hoping that this would end the blackmail. But it was only the beginning.

Stage 4 – Ben's Breakdown

Ben kept all this a complete secret from his family and friends over the course of four weeks after making the first payment to Emma.

He continued to pay up whenever Emma demanded, which was every 2-3 days and about the same amount each time, in the region of £250-£300. This continued until Ben had no money left in his account.

During this time everything about Ben changed. His mood and relationships at home nosedived. He became quiet and withdrew almost completely from family life. Instead of enjoying evenings with his parents and sister, he locked himself away in his room. He became snappy with his replies if any of his family asked him a question.

Ben withdrew from his friendship group too, both online and in the real world. He wouldn't turn up to football training, he didn't go out in the evenings or weekends to any event, whether it was a birthday or the cinema or just to hang out. His friends were surprised by this drastic change in his personality, so they alerted his family.

Ben's schoolwork also suffered. He didn't get his assignments or homework done, lost all concentration, and withdrew from any class interaction and participation. His teachers wrote home to explain the turn of events at school. Whenever they approached Ben, he would deflect their questions and tell them that "everything is okay".

The final straw that broke Ben and led to him pushing his mum, and eventually to me getting involved in the case, was when Ben said he had no more money to give Emma. Emma insisted he find some more money. She said if he paid a final sum of £1000 he could end all this and she'd delete all the videos and pictures.

Ben had absolutely no money left and felt that his world was crumbling. He didn't know where to turn and was completely lost. His brain was swimming with fear and self-criticism, as he beat himself up about his "stupidity". Here are some of his thoughts and feelings:

- How could he possibly get past this moment in his life – this was everything!
- His status among his family and friends would surely be ruined and he could never get that back.
- What would he be known as?
- How could he possibly look at his friends again without them thinking about "stupid Ben"; that he was the "idiot" that sent naked selfies to a "random" and got caught, literally with his pants down.
- He felt utter shame.
- He was embarrassed by his actions, and to confess this to his parents was terrifying.
- He felt completely worthless.
- Worse still, he felt duped into sending those explicit videos to 'Emma' in reply to her poorly crafted and blurry videos.

The devastating bubble that Ben was in finally burst when his father barged his way into Ben's room the day that he pushed his mum. As awful as things were, Ben felt a degree of relief to be able to share what had happened.

Stage 5 – Ben's Grieving

When I first spoke to Ben shortly after my scene-setting call with Mike, he explained that he was struggling with every part of his life and didn't know what to do. He was distraught about what he had done and how "stupid" he felt. He knew he should have done something about it much earlier, that he should have reached out to his mum and dad, but he was so embarrassed and ashamed of what he had been manipulated into, he couldn't bear to face his parents.

His feelings of utter shame and anxiety about being caught were so overwhelming that they consumed every waking moment of Ben's days. He was so scared that someone would find out and that he would be ridiculed, that he would be the laughingstock of his school, that he wouldn't be able to face his friends again. The intensity of his feelings led him to think about taking his own life.

Picture 2. Swallow Me Up

He told me he wanted the ground to open up and swallow him. Ben kept talking about what others would think of him, and how his decisions would cost him his future.

We spent time reviewing and reframing what had happened. It was important to get Ben to understand that he was a victim of a very carefully crafted business, designed to lure young men just like him. This was a cold-hearted operation in which each part of the strategy was meticulously executed to obtain the optimum desired outcome. They just wanted his money and were using his images and videos as a bargaining chip to ensure they got their money's worth.

Stage 6 – Online Reality?

It was essential that Ben understood that Emma was not "a real person". Emma was played by multiple young women in this deceit.

The method of operation of these groups currently appears to adhere to the following formula:

1. Access a friendship group – usually people in their teens or twenties.

2. Create as many friendships as possible with the male figures in the group.
3. Be actively involved in the group, posting pictures and commenting.
4. Start individual conversations with several of the male members in the group.
5. Gain their trust over a short period of time.
6. Coax them into an intimate online relationship by flirting and turning up the intensity of the conversation.
7. Start sending gently seductive pictures of themselves (either blurry or not fully including their face).
8. Request pictures of their prey, insisting on clear shots including the full face.
9. Start sending videos and gradually make them more explicit, asking for the same in return.
10. Promise to act out the videos in person when they meet.
11. Demand more sexually explicit videos and pictures, threatening to walk away from the relationship if they don't materialise.
12. Once they have enough content, demand that the victim pays blackmail money, or else the videos and pictures will be posted in all the friendship groups, posted to family and handed out in the school/college/university/workplace.
13. Once all funds are exhausted, demand a final "completion" payment from the victim, saying all content will then be destroyed.
14. Continue this strategy until they can no longer squeeze funds out of their victim.
15. Move on to the next victim.

This exploitation continues as long as payments are made. If the victim stops payment, the blackmailers generally (but not always) stop and move on to the next target. It is a tried and tested business model. The criminals doing it don't have an ounce of care or empathy for their victims. As soon as these schemes are found out and shut down, they set up another one. It is easy money and there's plenty of easy prey like Ben out there in the online world.

Ben's Reasoning

Why did Ben do this in the first place?

At that moment in his life, being socially accepted by his inner circle was of the utmost importance. Ben wanted nothing more than to have a girlfriend. All his mates had girlfriends. He was a good-looking guy, full of fun, sporty and positive to be around. Ben was always asking himself why was it that all his friends had girlfriends while he didn't.

As a teenager Ben's number one priority was to fit in. His mates would get together in couples and go out in groups – he would always be the odd one out.

He would get mocked by his mates and that would make him feel quite down. He began spending hours hidden in his bedroom late at night scouring social media and influencers, researching how to get a girlfriend. The fallout from the blue-light sessions had huge effects on his life; not enough sleep, missing college, reduced quality of judgement, irritability, and spinning thoughts from the content of his late-night binges.

The fear of missing out (FoMO)[2] was so intense that it made Ben "desperate". This took away all rationality in his normal judgements and that's where he slipped up. He was so desperate for that feeling of belonging that all the alarm bells that would normally ring were silenced, especially when he saw that a "really pretty" girl was showing interest in him. This was what he had been waiting for, and here she was, in the palm of his hands. Unfortunately, he didn't realise he was being played.

Ben's intense need for belonging, to have a girlfriend, to be seen as "one of the boys", blinded him when he needed clarity and rational decision-making most. This blind spot helped his predators lure him into their honey trap. They enticed him perfectly, influencing a change in his behaviour, and just when he thought he was a "winner" he was brought back down to Earth with an almighty crash. He was then extorted in a way that is desperately saddening, because Ben, like many others, was ill-equipped to deal with this level of sophistication.

Shutting Down the Predators

I worked with Ben, Mike and Andrea to create an overall strategy to tackle the problem. It followed a step-by-step process to ensure Ben's safety – it was crucial to shut down Emma and the predator team to reduce their threat.

We tackled many different issues concurrently. Some were practical steps that had to be completed, and others focused on improving the emotional state of each of the three.

We started off by reporting Emma to the social media companies and notifying the police. This was the fastest and most effective way of closing down Emma and the channels they were using to inflict pain. The police added this complaint to their long list of investigations of this type. Emma's account was immediately blocked and removed by the social media companies, and they sent the relevant data to the police who opened a case for the incident.

This was the most important step as it removed the overhanging threat, anxiety, stress and pressure that had built up in Ben. It allowed him to breathe without the fear of being "exposed" to his friends and family and potentially having his "life ruined".

The police sent officers round to discuss the situation and collate as much information and evidence as possible on Emma and the group she was working with. The police were very empathetic towards Ben and explained that many situations like this were reported to them daily. They assured Ben that none of this was his fault. They told him he was up against a machine which was very powerful and had limitless resources available because it was such a lucrative, nasty business.

At the same time, we worked on the intense emotions that Ben, Mike and Andrea were feeling. Ben was carrying a tremendous amount of deep shame, guilt and anger after the ordeal. We looked at the reasons for this, then worked on reframing his views about the entire misadventure by using different coaching and NLP (Neuro-Linguistic Programming)[3] techniques.

Ben worked hard to lessen the power of the damaging feelings he was grappling with and to normalise what had happened. He understood and accepted that he only represented money to Emma, and that this was about just one thing: the extortion and blackmail of any subject they could entice.

I also helped Mike and Andrea to explore their emotions and reframe what had happened. They focused some of their efforts on understanding their own feelings of anger, shame and frustration at not stepping in to help Ben at an earlier stage. They had no idea the blackmail was happening, and that was what hurt and affected them the most. They had believed that their relationship with Ben was open and trusting enough that he would confide in them no matter what.

It was evident that Mike and Andrea wished they'd acted earlier, as soon as they became aware of Ben's moods and change in personality, and that something must have been very wrong. They had clear red flags in the form of enquiries from Ben's friends and teachers – all of them concerned about the sudden change in Ben's personality.

Looking back at the events as they unfolded, Mike and Andrea were critical of themselves for not intervening earlier, which would have prevented the prolonged pain that Ben endured.

The intervention only came about by sheer chance, due to Ben's aggressive outburst. What would have happened if things hadn't played out that way? This is a question Andrea and Mike worked through as they didn't want anything of this kind to happen to their family again. Consequently, they created a "safe zone" in their home where anything and everything could be discussed openly, without confrontation, without judgement, ensuring care, consideration and empathy. The change since the implementation of the "safe zone" has been extremely positive for their individual and combined relationships.

Conclusion

Luckily this situation was brought to an end before it became catastrophic for Ben and his family. The financial loss was certainly difficult to stomach, but nowhere near as bad as what could have happened if the intervention hadn't taken place when it did.

The intervention allowed Ben to take a moment to pause, understand that he was in a safe space, surrounded by love and care, and fortunate to have a family that was determined to help.

I need to point out that Mike's aggressive response is not what I would recommended to any parent, carer or guardian – it could have gone disastrously wrong and caused far more pain and devastation. In this case, the tactics Mike used to shake Ben out of his anxiety and inability to see a way forward, worked – but my experience suggests that this type of approach rarely works.

There has to be a progressive, careful response to situations like Ben's, otherwise it can tip them over the edge.

What happened to Ben, and could happen to any teenager, male or female, was a masterful display of misrepresentation, distortion, distraction, extortion and blackmail at its most brutal. There is a script that these gangs have perfected and use on countless teens across the world. It is created in different languages, reflecting the cultural nuances of the country concerned, to reel in unsuspecting and vulnerable victims. These gangs prey on children who are longing for acceptance and belonging, and as such are easy targets.

This is a numbers game. These gangs operate on multiple victims simultaneously, extorting money from many young people. It's a very profitable factory.

The social media companies know this happens but choose not to act – they consider it to be too much effort for them to police. Their standard public response is that everything is encrypted so they can't know what's going on unless it is reported to them first. By their default we are forced to police this ourselves, and many parents are currently ill-equipped to do so.

It happens all over the world, and will not stop happening until we all, adults and children, become aware of the dangers that are lurking, staying alert and mindful of the bad actors that want to inflict pain for financial gain.

In Ben's case, he fell headfirst into their honey trap and paid the price by emptying his bank balance into their pockets.

Ben has come to terms with what happened and has processed the shame, stress, anxiety and depression. He's now looking forward to a positive, happy, purposeful and fulfilling life.

Mike and Andrea have worked through their own emotions and thoughts surrounding the painful experience and are glad to have intervened at least when they did. They have, together, moved on with a stronger and more open family relationship, with trust, honesty, sharing and empathy at its core.

Rebel Insights Tips – Help Protect from Extortion and Blackmail

1. Make sure that all your social media channels are set at private.
2. Make sure to block and / or ignore any connections from strangers.
3. Do not move to a different social media platform if asked by someone you don't know.
4. Do not start a video chat with anyone you don't know.

5. A photo or a video of a new connection who you don't know is not proof that they are who they say they are; this could be an avatar or a front for a group looking to extort money from you.
6. Do not send any photos or videos of yourself in any form that could compromise you.
7. Do not send any nude photographs or videos of yourself to anyone, EVER!
8. If anyone is trying to extort money from you, please report this to a loved one, to the police, and to the platform you use to communicate with this person.
9. Keep all evidence; do not delete! Make sure you download all messages, pictures, video, and any other interaction so that it can be used by law enforcement.
10. Any image of you that has been uploaded can be removed by request to the following organisation: The Internet Watch Foundation, a UK charity set up to help remove sexual images and videos of under 18s posted online:

    www.iwf.org.uk/our-technology/report-remove/

11. Please remember that as embarrassing or frightening, stressful or devastating as this may be, you're not the only one that this is happening to. You are not alone; it happens to many other people, and there is always a solution, a way out to something that is more positive.
12. Parents – stay strong, be resilient, and create an open, safe and caring environment for your children to converse.
13. Adopt active listening skills. Never confront and never judge, just be fully present with empathy, care, love and kindness.

If you would like to know more about becoming a parent-coach for your children and avoiding, preventing, and intervening with addictive screen tendencies, click on the QR code below for the Rebel Therapies website where you can also find various helpful downloadable information sheets and top tips which are covered through this book.

Chapter 3

Gamification

Gaming is becoming a new normal for younger and younger children, with them being exposed to content that is way beyond their viewing age! Why do we allow our children to take part in online games that are not suitable for them? Are we as desensitised as they are? In our minds, are the new 15 or 18 age classifications now the new U or PG classifications?

Online gaming is big business and is getting bigger! Gaming companies are continually coming up with new, cleverly incentivised ways to entice and con our children out of billions of pounds and dollars each year – and we are letting it happen on our watch!

I want to introduce you to one of my recent case studies about a young boy called Pete. This case study outlines what happened to Pete and his family when gamification[1] took hold, the consequences of Pete's actions and what we did to change their relationships both with technology and with each other.

When I first found out about Pete he was 12 years old, and he'd been playing Fortnite for nearly two years. Pete's mother reached out to me in the summer of 2022 and explained there was a massive problem with her son and his addiction to gaming.

Pete was an avid and enthusiastic gamer! He had been playing games, first on a PS4 and then a PS5. His dad, Ian, introduced Pete to gaming when he was about 18 months old. Pete would sit and watch Ian play games and eventually learnt to hold a controller and play the same games that his dad was playing. It used to be fun, and they used to play most of the games together, right up to the point where his father got bored of the games. Pete didn't get bored of them, though.

Pete was extremely competitive when he played online games with his friends, and often asked his parents if he could upgrade and update his guns and cars, and do anything else that was needed to improve his gaming experience.

He would get the extra bits that he needed to add extensions on all the weaponry and armour, or new tyres, or a new wing – whatever add-ons he needed – and he had to have the best.

With these types of games, you often need to spend hours and hours playing. It can take days, weeks or even months to complete the multiple levels required to gain in-house credits to afford these desired add-ons. The term "credits" encompasses coins, credits, bucks and any other in-app purchasing capabilities.

The add-ons in most of these games are quite expensive. For instance, when playing a game like DragonVale, if you want to get a new egg for a new dragon you've collected, you've got to pay! If it's a rare egg, you need to spend a lot of your credits. It takes an awfully long time to build up that level of credit in your bank.

Picture 1. Coins, Credits, Bucks

In addition to the extremely high price tags for these games, gaming companies force the concept of "gamification" upon their users. The inordinate length of time it takes to build up credits in your piggy bank is purposefully designed to create an environment of temptation. It is difficult for unsuspecting users to not succumb to in-app purchasing. Their needing to buy additional credits to top up their piggy bank to enhance the enjoyment of their game can be overwhelming.

We can quite clearly link gamification with the science of behavioural change rewards systems. The idea of winning or buying credits creates a massive rush in the brain – it induces a full-on dopamine hit! This dopamine-fuelled response creates craving, and that craving creates an even greater desire to get more credits, to be able to buy more add-ons and create more options in your gameplay. Players of these games, buyers of these credits, are feeding their addictive tendencies, and are using the argument of wanting to be better at the game – more effective, faster, stronger or powerful, to gain more kudos within their friendship and online groups – either as an excuse or to mask their addiction, whether they are consciously aware of this or not.

For a 12-year-old child like Pete, it's particularly important to keep up with your friends, especially if they are all playing the same online game, in the same environment and looking to play against each other. Being the best means you have bragging rights! Bragging rights can bring fame in your own small world. Even if it is just your group of friends, you may want to stand out, show that you are more capable, and that you have more buying power than anybody else around you! Many children lack control and confidence in their real off-line lives, so the online world gives them an environment where they can experience self-worth, respect, and control of their destinies. But this is not real control; it is created by escapism, and in some cases, it is an attempt to escape from very difficult situations and environments the children experience in their real world.

My work in this area of gaming and the online world which I liken to the Wild West, has highlighted that some parents don't really know what is happening to their children. They don’t necessarily understand the constant pressure, need, and desire to fit in with the other kids, to show that they are equal – to not be bullied or have the mickey taken out of them, to be seen as worthy within their fragile friendship groups. It’s exhausting at the best of times, particularly with the way technology dominates so much of how our children live today.

The best way I know to learn and understand what is happening in their worlds is to be fully present, in constant communication with them and to use the strategy of “active listening” at every opportunity.

Reaching Out – An Intervention

Pete's mother, Helen, reached out to me because she needed an immediate intervention! Her son had managed to persuade his parents to put their credit card details onto his PS5 so he could pay for his yearly PS5 subscription, allowing him to log in to play games, download free games, and be present in the online community with his other friends. What they didn't realise was the extent of in-app purchasing that would occur.

The jaw-dropping headline Helen told me was that in a matter of only a couple of weeks Pete had spent £9,000 on in-app purchasing!

Helen only found out about the huge spend when she was out with some girlfriends for a dinner. At the end of the night when Helen went to pay her portion of the bill, her credit card was rejected. Helen didn't have a clue that it was because her son had happily spent it all on in-app purchases.

Helen told me that she immediately called the credit card company to find out why her credit had been blocked. When Helen was told the reason, her friends noticed the blood drain from her face as she turned white. The credit card company told her that she had already reached her £10,000 limit for the month.

In complete shock and disbelief, she argued with the credit card company, saying that it was impossible, there was no way that she could have spent £10,000 in this month, or any month – that the most she had spent was £1,000.

When Helen asked the credit card company to explain what the money had been spent on, she was told it had been paid to several technology companies in the United States. Helen wracked her brain to think how this was possible and her first thought was that it had to be a terrible mistake … that something had gone incredibly wrong somewhere but that it could be easily resolved. Her second thought, which she described as coming from deep within her gut, was that it was linked to her son, but she didn't want to believe that. She absolutely didn't want to face the fact that her son could have spent £9,000 online. The credit card company said there was no mistake on their part, and that the money had gone out in five major chunks over a two-week period.

When Helen finished the phone call with the credit card company, she immediately called home and relayed the story to her husband Ian, who was similarly shocked and devastated upon hearing the news.

Meanwhile, Helen had to retain a brave face in front of her friends, while she tried to get to the bottom of this credit card bombshell. She asked Ian to go and check with her son to see if he had in fact purchased anything in the Fortnite game he was playing, or if they were completely wrong. Helen was still hoping that it wasn't the case, and that it was all a terrible mistake. However, something inside told her that her son had probably created this massive issue without fully understanding the catastrophic impact it would have on them as a family.

Helen explained to me that she felt terribly embarrassed in front of her friends that night. She had never had a problem like this. In getting to know Helen over the last couple of years, it had become very clear to me that she was an immensely proud person and was feeling a great deal of shame. Because Helen was normally seen as the mother figure, the "sensible one" in her friendship group, her self-concept further compounded the stress and perceived enormity of her situation, as she also found it difficult and shameful to ask her friends to pay for her dinner.

In my first ever conversation with Helen, she told me that the topic of gaming had already been quite contentious within her family unit. The amount of time that her son Pete spent playing his games, with the blessing of her husband, was causing deep stress, frustration and anger. She was very much against it; however, they could never really find common ground or a unified way of showing their son that his gaming habit was too much, and terribly out of balance. Helen labelled it "an addiction" rather than just a love of gaming. It was probably both of these things, because love for gaming and addiction can easily go hand in hand, as you are bathed in dopamine, the pleasure hormone, when playing games.

Shame On Me!

In our subsequent conversations, Helen returned to that moment quite often as she tried to work through her harrowing emotions and practised reframing techniques to deal with the painful memories of that night. The conversation with her husband, and trying to hide her distress from her friends, were among the most difficult moments in her life. For Helen, showing her fragility was a definite "no-no" and it fuelled her overwhelm.

It caused tremendous stress for Helen, not just at that moment but over time. While her friends came to the rescue and magnanimously paid her bill, Helen could not let go of the utter shame and worthlessness she felt as a parent, that this could happen to her!

Helen felt that she had lost standing in her friendship group. She felt judged for her son's actions and the inexcusable inaction of her husband. Sensing that she was being laughed at for what was happening in her family unit, and that she had no control over it, was crippling for Helen.

So not only was this a financial problem for Helen. There was a significant emotional and physical element too.

The impact on her body, brain and emotional wellbeing was bruising. Together we explored the situation to unpack the spectrum of emotions that had taken a physical toll on Helen during the intervening months between the night of her friends' dinner and our sessions. While we made good progress, we were yet to address the impact of the experience within her family unit.

Helen's friends were really supportive in the immediate aftermath of Helen's financial shock. However this did little to balance the distress Helen experienced as she fought to recover the cost of Pete's spending spree. The gaming companies took absolutely no responsibility, and provided no duty of care when Helen reached out and asked them if they would help refund some or all of the £9,000. Helen pointed out the ease with which her son was able to purchase thousands of pounds worth of stuff in his games. She explained that as far as she knew, at no point were there any recommendations or alerts that popped up to warn her and her husband of the specific nature of these purchases. The gaming company said it was their own fault and liability, and that they should have known.

In our first call Helen questioned how she could possibly have known about the devastating nature of in-app purchasing – she had never been exposed to it before.

How Could Helen Know?

Usually when Helen paid for something on her phone, a notification would appear. However, any purchases not made on her phone went unnoticed until she checked her statement at the end of each month, when she religiously performed her reconciliation.

Therefore, the purchases her son made were not seen in time. If they were, she could have immediately stopped the withdrawals as soon as she saw the first purchase go through, realising it wasn't something that she had agreed to. The credit card company, just like the gaming companies, told Helen that it was her own fault – she had given her son the pin number and therefore had authorised the purchases. The credit card company explained that if the correct procedures were followed, they could not stop a payment from going through, and could only issue a refund if fraud had been committed against her. They pointed out that it could have been her husband or herself who made the purchases – how were they to know?

There are restrictions on playtime and also how much money you can spend on most games, including Fortnite, so that once you have spent a certain amount of time playing, they switch off. Or if you spend up to your limit, you can no longer make purchases, unless you manually override it.

The purchases didn't happen just once but multiple times. It is important to highlight Helen's story as there don't appear to be any clear guidelines on what to look out for as a parent when it comes to children playing online games where in-app purchasing is automatically set to 'On' as part of their factory settings.

The painful truth is that similar issues will continue to arise unless the game companies are forced to make the guidelines for in-app purchasing more transparent. The unfortunate fact is that organisations who create these games are not required or incentivised to start the game with a zero default. It is not in their financial interests to give parents the power to choose purchasing limits.

My suggestion which I will continue to put forward to these gaming companies is that there should be a zero in-app purchasing default when the game is first downloaded, whether you're playing on a PS5, an Xbox, iPad, or similar alternative.

Helen's dreadful experience is not uncommon. Anyone reading this chapter who thinks that it could never happen to them might want to think twice. I recommend putting in place checks and balances in the home to ensure this doesn't become reality.

You need to ensure that as a parent, guardian, or caregiver, you are checking in with your children, and that you're aware of what they are doing when playing these games. Put limits on. Switch off the in-app capability. Anyone with a child under 18 needs to monitor their child's online usage. Make it explicit and obtain agreement from the other adults in the family unit. If you don't do this, you're opening up yourself and your family to the possibility of harm.

Concentrate On Pete – For Pete's Sake!

During my time working with Helen, we agreed that I would work with Pete, but only if he agreed and wanted to change his behaviour with regard to screens and his gaming addiction.

Pete was a typical, energetic 12-year-old boy who loved to play games. Always excited about playing with his friends online, how he could do things better, what he could do to overcome the obstacles of a particular level or in a particular game, and always wanting to be the best.

Pete had no real insight or understanding of the impact of his in-app spending spree.

When I spoke with Pete directly, I could tell that he didn't really understand the pain that his actions could cause, and he made it clear to me that there were no rules governing his gameplay.

In fact his dad, Ian, encouraged it. The lines of communication between Pete and his parents were "all over the place". None of their messages made sense; none of it helped shape clear and defined guidelines that were necessary for Pete.

Pete had effectively been given an open chequebook. Pete mentioned he was even encouraged by his dad to play online games and told not to bother him when the two of them were at home on their own. He told me that his dad would "do endless scrolling on his phone and watch videos on YouTube for hours" when Helen was out. This allowed Pete to sit with his PS5 and play continuously with no parental interaction or interruption.

Pete was open and honest with me and told me that he would have preferred to play board games, or kick a ball, or do something else, but that his dad was never really into it. Whenever they had their "boy time", when Helen went out, Pete would initially suggest doing something else, but would be guided to play online because his "dad was too tired". Pete explained he would initially get frustrated and annoyed as he didn't want to spend all day playing online. However, as time went by, Pete was content to go online and play his games. The consistent messaging by Ian gently changed Pete's behaviour over time, and that change effectively took over his life.

When I asked Pete how he felt about his in-app purchasing and what he thought about while going through that process, his response was quite interesting. Pete was not at all concerned about making those purchases as he didn't see it as real money. It was all just credits to him, so once he got into the flow of buying more skins, or more ammunition or weapons, whatever it was, it was just Fortnite credits (V-Bucks). These V-Bucks held no monetary value in Pete's eyes at the time. He told me that he went on a spending spree and would talk to his friends, who would persuade him to buy something better … a more expensive and impressive skin. This drove Pete forward with energy and onto a two-week purchasing extravaganza!

When I asked Pete what he felt when he found out that he had spent £9,000 of his parents' money, which they didn't have, he just slumped in his seat and he looked down at the ground, fiddling with his fingers. Then he said, "I'm sorry, I'm sorry for what I did – I didn't know." He went on to tell me that if he'd understood the implications of his actions he wouldn't have gone so "crazy" and bought everything that was available.

Pete mentioned quite quickly in that first conversation that "it's wrecked home life". He told me that his mum and dad were having "quite a difficult time", that they spent a lot of time arguing with each other. Most of the arguments were about their parenting responsibilities – the rules and the boundaries that they should have in place with Pete. Pete was seeing, hearing, feeling all his parents' anger and frustrations through the viewpoint of an adolescent. Pete told me he started to hate himself. He thought he was solely responsible for all the problems happening within his family. That is a terrible burden for a young child to bear. Pete was the recipient of indifferent and indecisive parenting and should not have had to bear the responsibility of his actions. To feel that he was solely to blame for his parents' anguish was really tough on Pete.

Pete was just doing what a child does. Pete was not an adult. At the age of 12 Pete still had at least another 12 years of his life before his brain would be fully mature. The prefrontal cortex[2], the front part of the brain that helps you make rational decisions, and understand the consequences of those decisions, doesn't mature until you are about 25.

As a 12-year-old who's been given free rein and has been able to do whatever he wants without any real guidance, Pete could not be the target of blame. The inability of Helen and Ian to discuss the issue privately and agree a way forward in terms of how they brought up their child, what they did and did not expect as parents, and what they modelled to their child, was not Pete's fault in any way.

I asked Pete if it was okay for me to share what he said to me with his parents. It was vital for them to understand Pete's thoughts and feelings, especially the deep level of blame he was holding on to. Their new awareness could encourage Helen and Ian to compromise and create a united front going forward when teaching their son. They needed to learn how to stand together and show agreement with each other, instead of disputing decisions in front of Pete.

Time for Change!

To bring about positive change in the family's relationships with technology, screens and each other, we implemented an agreed strategy which was split into three stages.

The first stage centred on my discussions specifically with Helen. The second stage was directed at my interactions with Pete. The third stage was focused on my discussions with Helen and Ian.

The aim of the first stage was to understand the problems from Helen's perspective. Why was it that they had consulted me? What was the core issue? What was Helen's highest positive outcome of this intervention and working with me? Was there an easy fix? Why was technology so addictive? Would it be possible to break free of its hold over her family? How could Helen get her husband on board and change?

The second stage involved interacting with Pete, understanding what he knew, what he thought, and to get deep knowledge of his perspectives. This meant creating various levels of self-awareness for Pete and enabling him to process why his parents were deeply upset about what had happened.

We also worked on changing the landscape at home and explored the root causes of Pete's addiction to gaming.

The third stage involved working with both parents so they could provide a unified front when they were delivering any kind of messaging and boundaries, or anything related to reward or punishment for their son. We also worked on understanding their own relationship, why they did what they did, why they never had the conversation about being unified, and what the benefits of a unified approach would look like.

We don't need to always wholly agree with our partners regarding how we bring up our children. However, we do need to compromise on what that looks like. If you have a unified approach you will have a better outcome. It is not always going to be easy, and you may not always be right, but nevertheless you create certainty and clear boundaries of what is and is not acceptable.

Rebel Insights Tip 1 – Unified Approach

Try not to disagree with each other in front of your children if it's about the way you're bringing your children up. You can disagree about political parties, what movies you like, what football teams you support, and you can disagree on whether something is tasty or not tasty, but in terms parenting – rewarding, disciplining and helping your children grow – you need to have a unified approach.

Rebel Insights Tip 2 – Gaming Contract

Agree a gaming contract with your children. It's invaluable. I suggest the contract includes the following:

- How often they play for – for example two times a week after school
- How long they play for – set exact times such as 5pm-6pm
- What games they're allowed to play – be explicit as to what games are acceptable. I suggest using age limits on games as a reference point for agreement.

- Agree what is acceptable with in-app purchasing. I would strongly advise setting this at £0 and keeping it there!

There must be gaming rules put in place with full agreement from all parties: children and adults. If those rules are not abided by, and the contract isn't foolproof, and isn't implemented fully, then it's as good as wet toilet roll!

Rebel Insights Tip 3 – Emotional Targets

As well as setting timing controls, you also need to set emotional targets. You need to be explicit with your child regarding aggressive behaviour. They need to agree to starting and stopping playing any online game in a positive manner. Do not allow any wriggle room where your child ends a gaming session in an angry state. There is to be no aggression when they stop playing the game. If they are unable to stick to this agreement, the game needs to be confiscated for a period of time. This is normally set up in the gaming contract agreement.

Helen and Ian's relationship initially took a real battering from what happened with Pete. Helen's father bailed them out and paid the full credit card debt. It was heaven-sent as Helen and Ian could not afford to pay it off themselves. He kindly said he would never ask for it to be repaid, but stressed that it was an unfortunate and extremely expensive lesson for them to learn as a family.

Conclusion

At our latest review, Pete was 14. He had a highly active life with sports, friends, and more fun time with his mum and dad that didn't involve screens.

Helen came to terms with the pain and suffering that she felt during the six months after she found out about Pete's spending spree, and worked hard to create a happier and healthier lifestyle with her family. She was also relieved, and forever appreciative of her father's charity in clearing the gaming debt.

Helen and her husband had forged a much stronger relationship and were better aligned in how they coached Pete. They had listened, learnt, accepted advice, and worked through some of the fundamental issues they had in their relationship to be able to create a togetherness in how they delivered to Pete, which is so important moving forward.

We will continue to work together as new challenges face them, especially with the Wild West of the online world. For now, they hope that their story can be a lesson learned in what not to do, and precautions you can take to avoid similar mistakes with in-app purchasing.

Online gamification and in-app purchasing is a massive business and represents a significant proportion of the profitability of gaming companies. It is in their interest to get you and your children hooked on those games and paying for additions. These companies want you to spend, spend, spend!

Picture 2. Daylight Robbery!

There is no legislative, internal or external requirement for them to think about their users' mental, physical or financial wellbeing. Whatever restrictions or warnings that they may claim to have in their games, they are not as effective as putting in a default of zero, or a no-spend default. They want to make it as easy as possible for you to spend. Wouldn't it be refreshing if the default was set to zero, and if you wanted to make a purchase you had to actively go through the process of putting in all your credit card details each time you decided to buy!

They don't want to do that. In-app purchasing needs to be seamless and easy, and as close to 1-click purchasing as possible. Their strategy involves behavioural science at its most dangerous – to not allow you to think twice before you commit and buy!

Rebel Insights Tip 4 – Parental Approval for All In-App Purchases

Resist!! Resist the temptation to switch on any online in-app purchasing capability. Discuss the perils of in-app purchasing with your children.

Rebel Insights Tip 5 – Don't Share Your Credit Card

My final top tip is quite clearly: Do not give them your credit card details or your pin number – just say "NO."

Please scan the QR code below for the Rebel Insights page at www.RebelTherapies.com where you can find the tips mentioned in this book along with various other downloadable information.

Chapter 4

Online Babysitter

Is the addictive pull of our devices turning us into zombies, aimlessly following each other into oblivion? The constant dopamine our brains receive from our devices impacts us severely, but none more so than the group we need to protect most in their early years. Our children are fair game and the most vulnerable to digital devices and content. The damage to their brains[1] and the negative impact on their behaviour is evident in my clients' children as illustrated in this case study.

A Cry For Help

I first found out about Kate when I received a text from her mother Pam. The text just read:

> *"Help. I can't get my children off YouTube.*
> *Please call me."*

Pam and her husband Lee had two children. When Pam was introduced to me through a friend of a friend, their daughter Kate was five years old, and their son Toby was two. Pam explained that Lee was away quite often on business, either in the Far East or in the US, which left Pam feeling like she was "living as a single mother". Pam would be at home on her own for days if not weeks looking after a very demanding daughter and an inquisitive little boy. Pam also worked part-time as a teaching assistant in the primary school her daughter attended. Her son was still too young to go to school and usually spent his days with Pam's parents when Pam was working.

Both Pam and Lee grew up in middle-class English families. They were financially stable, and while Pam didn't have to work, she valued the mental and social stimulation it offered, rather than "just staying at home" looking after her young children.

When Pam and I first met over a Zoom call, I really wanted to find out more about their family dynamic, and the couple's general parenting strategy. My intention was to get a clear picture of their current state, and to create a baseline to measure against, so we could monitor the progress we made as we worked together. I wanted to understand their general house rules, their values and boundaries, how they parented their children, and why Pam had sent me the original text message – her initial cry for help.

Pam described a desperate situation. What was interesting in this case was the gradual escalation of household screen usage that coincided with her children's behavioural problems. Understanding Pam and Lee's respective childhoods would help me to gauge how some of their values and beliefs were shaped and carried into their own parenting formula.

As an only child, Pam recalled having anything and everything that she wanted or needed, and her parents almost never said "No" to her. When we explored her upbringing, Pam realised she grew up with an idyllic view of life in a privileged environment where she never dealt with the disappointment of not having something. This background information helped me to understand how Pam's issues became so drastic and why she reached out for help.

Because Pam's childhood requests had never been rejected and most of the people in her life had never told her "No", she had only one way of viewing the ideal way of bringing up a child, and that was always to say "Yes". It was clear that she could not instinctively assess situations and decide which times her children probably shouldn't do or have something, and then manage the consequences of that decision. It appeared that Pam's upbringing meant that she missed out on some of those uncomfortable experiences which would have instilled the ability to measure what the most appropriate response would be for both the short-term and long-term benefit of her family ecosystem.

I mention rational decision-making and behaviour frequently in this book, as I believe it's one of the most crucial concepts in understanding our children and their own decision-making capacity. It allows us to fully appreciate why children do what they do, the actions they take, and the repercussions that follow.

As we grow up, we might learn social skills such as turn-taking, kindness and empathy, and other rules for successful social interaction. These behaviours help us interact with other people and teach us that actions have consequences. We take actions and make decisions all the time, and I would argue that some people make "better" decisions than others.

Why is that the case? How do some of us seem to easily make the "right" decision, and arrive at the most responsible, well thought-out course of action while others don't? This is primarily down to the way we have been wired during the early years of life. Our ability to make rational decisions and understand the consequences of those decisions and behaviours is formed throughout our childhood and adolescent life. We acquire this ability by observing and learning from those closest to us – our parents, siblings, extended family, friends, teachers and other role models.

As we battle with the consequences of our decisions and actions – as we move through the stages of adolescence and into our late teens and early twenties – we create long-lasting neural pathways in our brain, specifically in an area at the front of our brains called the prefrontal cortex.

We use these synaptic pathways[2] when solving problems, making rational decisions, and considering their costs and benefits. If our prefrontal cortex does not have a properly developed set of synapses, we may tend to make poor decisions and then suffer as a result. To become properly developed, our prefrontal cortex needs to learn from what happens when we engage in 'risky' play and behaviour,[1] from when we are born to our mid-twenties. If we miss out on the learning from those risky experiences, those synapses cannot strengthen and deepen enough to formulate the necessary neural pathways in our prefrontal cortex. We may then continually make poorly judged decisions and have a reduced ability to recognise behavioural consequences because we do not have the neural foundations of a rational approach.

With this science in mind, I draw your attention to Pam and Lee, and ask you to think about their decision-making, which had the effect of allowing their children to be glued to screens from morning till night.

Pause For Reflection

I would like to pause and ask you to reflect on what you've learnt so far. With your own children in mind, try to answer the following questions:

- What balance do your children have between screen usage and non-screen experiences?
- What is the impact of the one-way traffic from the screens to your children's young, underdeveloped brains?
- What manipulation may be happening to your children online?
- How empathetic are your children?

- Do you notice any difference between their behaviour after screen time and after time spent in personal interaction?

How Did It Get So Bad?

Pam first introduced the iPad to her daughter, Kate, when she was just shy of a year old. Pam said she did this because she was dead tired most of the time, and that Kate was way too energetic for her to deal with. Pam mentioned that she had never fully recovered from her pregnancy. To make things more difficult for Pam, she was quite alone and had no extended family to lean on for help. At the time, Pam's parents weren't close by like they are now, and there was no one else on hand to help bring up her one-year-old. Her utter fatigue crippled her, and she found it very difficult to just get out of bed.

Pam told me she took handfuls of supplements and tried lots of different homoeopathic concoctions, tried yoga and other exercise, but she could never fully snap out of the fatigue that engulfed her. It seemed like the only way for Pam to keep her daughter quiet was to give her an iPad, stick on YouTube and let her watch episode after episode of *Peppa Pig* for hours at a time.

At Kate's most formative age, when she was most susceptible to influence, Pam single-handedly created her daughter's devotion and addiction to screens. As soon as Kate awoke she would be given two things:

1. A bottle with warm milk, and
2. A fully charged iPad

This became a normal part of the routine for the family, a ritual. Pam explained that even when Lee was back at home from working abroad, he would get up very early and would normally be the one who had the first interaction with Kate. Like *Groundhog*

Day,[3] he religiously fetched Kate her bottle and the fully charged iPad as he got ready to go to work. This situation was deliberately embedded by Pam and Lee for their own benefit, as explained in Pam's own words:

> *"We were completely out of control but also completely in control. I loved the peace and quiet it gave me. Not having to run around after her was heaven-sent. I just couldn't do it; I simply didn't have the energy. I look back at it now and wonder: how did it get so bad?"*

Pam and Lee didn't observe the negative effects this habit was having on Kate, and themselves, until their son Toby was born. Kate was three years old when Toby arrived. Even then, Pam told me they followed the same pattern; they would stick the iPad in front of Kate while Pam looked after their newborn son.

By the time Toby turned two he was as proficient with an iPad and an iPhone as his sister Kate. In fact, there were things that Toby had learnt to do on the devices that Kate couldn't.

From Bad To Worse!

The problems began in earnest when Kate started to attack her little brother when she thought it was her turn to have the iPad, even though she had been given a separate iPhone to use. Pam told me that they put in place a "sharing agreement" for the iPad with Kate and Toby. It was a loose agreement, and she told the kids they would need it in place if they wanted to use the iPad and iPhone. When one had the iPhone, the other would get the iPad, then after some time – which was not specified in their "sharing agreement" – they would swap devices. Their device usage per day was between five and eight hours.

Pam explained that Kate wasn't into sharing the iPad and always wanted it for herself. If she saw Toby with it and wanted it, she would take it from Toby. If Toby put up resistance or sought to get it back, all hell would break loose and Kate would mount a full-on attack by hitting him with a hard object, usually a toy truck. Sometimes the exchanges would be so aggressive and so sudden that Pam would have no chance of getting in between Kate and Toby to protect her son. Kate would hit Toby on the head with such force that he bled, splitting his eyebrow, among other injuries.

On numerous occasions Pam had to take Toby to the Accident and Emergency Unit at their local hospital to get stitches in his head, such was the force and ferocity of Kate's attacks.

This was becoming increasingly worrying for both Pam and Lee, as well as Pam's parents, who told them they had to do something about their "crazy" situation and that it could not continue. Pam also clarified with me that both the iPad and iPhone were hers and not Kate's or Toby's, but they had complete rule over who used them.

Pam mentioned that whenever someone phoned her, she would rarely be allowed to speak to them, as the calls were always cancelled or ended because either Kate or Toby had the phone. If Pam wanted to answer the call, the kids would run riot. Pam explained that she had been attacked many times by either her son or her daughter. They would punch her, kick her, scratch her, and it would be unbearable … but she would always give in to their demands. She always gave in to her children!

It was becoming an impossible task, and she mentioned to me that both the hospital and the social services were very concerned about the frequency of injuries, and about the circumstances in the household which had allowed the situation to unfold. There was also a serious question mark over Lee's involvement – his attitude to all of this and how it had developed.

The emotional trauma sustained by Pam, Lee and their two children was severe and cannot be underestimated. Pam suffered an array of emotions including:

- Stress
- Anxiety
- Frustration
- Anger
- Despair
- Shame
- Sadness
- Guilt
- Hopelessness

Emotions Run High!

We began our work together by exploring the various emotions that Pam had encountered, from the moment she realised that her daughter was so desperately addicted to screens, to sitting in hospital with her son bleeding from his head and having to get stitches for the third time, to her husband's unwillingness to take some of the strain and be there for her when she needed it most, to blaming herself, her husband and also her parents for multiple things; from how she was brought up to the family's current lack of support.

Pam really struggled throughout this process. She initially found it difficult to accept that her decisions and actions precipitated these incidents; that she was complicit in creating an environment where her children's screen addiction manifested physical harm, because of her and Lee's blinding desire for peace and quiet.

However, the fundamental flaws in her strategy, in their joint parenting strategy, had led to severe behavioural issues for both children. Pam and Lee's marriage was struggling, and Pam's relationships with her parents, the school, and her children were all strained.

Pam admitted that this problem was like a poison spreading through the family. That poison gave rise to unwanted feelings which she felt ashamed of. She acknowledged that at certain times she felt "complete hate" towards her daughter and her husband. At times, the shame erupted into uncontrollable feelings of anger and aggression, and its overspill would be directed at each of them.

Pam admitted to throwing and smashing things like plates and glasses. She recalled one time when she pulled the iPad out of Kate's hands and smashed it down as hard as she could, right next to her. Pam explained that she was completely out of control and felt the only way that she could take back some control was to shock Kate and "to show her that I was the boss!"

I must caution that this type of behaviour and shock tactic doesn't work, and that it inevitably sets you up for failure. Such behaviour demonstrates to your children that this is an acceptable way to behave. Resorting to anger, violence and causing pain – whether direct or indirect, mental or physical – is not helpful. It just reinforces the idea that it is okay to be aggressive, violent and controlling to obtain your goal.

This is in fact what happened with Pam's daughter, and Pam's outbursts reinforced Kate's aggressive behaviour described earlier. Kate learned that by creating severe discomfort for her parents through harming her brother or creating an unwanted situation – like breaking something, throwing a tantrum or causing general unpleasantness – she would be rewarded.

This type of reinforcement is extremely damaging as the behaviour becomes second nature, ingrained in ongoing behavioural patterns. These piercing negative traits can cause harm throughout your life.

Such reinforcement intensifies those connections in the prefrontal cortex which set the way that you behave unconsciously.

Pam explained that they did not implement any real strong parental controls, and certainly would never discipline their children … not at any point. Looking back, Pam realised that this contributed enormously to the impossible situation they found themselves in.

What became evident in my conversations with each family member is that angry and aggressive behaviour was a normal and acceptable way of life in their household. From my conversations with Kate, I realised the way she behaved was an exact mirror image of the way her parents would treat the children and each other.

As I observed Pam, Lee and their children within their family dynamic, it was evident that their parenting techniques at every level had combined to set them up for failure. What they needed was strength and depth in their parental controls, discipline, strategy and tools to rebalance their life. Boundaries for what was right and wrong needed to be verbally and nonverbally expressed in a kind, open, safe, interactive, and non-confrontational way.

A Tactical Change

Having unpacked all of this through our deep exploration into the lives of the family, we were able to introduce and implement a new parenting strategy. My aim was to teach the parents to become coaches to their children.

We implemented the strategy in stages so that incremental changes had time to be accepted and embedded into the family's environment, and become the "new normal". We gave outlet to the emotions and reframed the beliefs around the previously contentious anchors[4] of the smartphone and iPad for each family member.

Stage 1 – Behavioural Change for the Parents

The first stage was designed to change Pam and Lee's behaviour towards screens, and how they used them in front of their children. It was paramount for the parents to be role models of "good" screen usage for their children. At the same time, we slowly reduced the physical presence of screens during the day for the children.

Primarily, I worked with Pam and Lee individually, to help them become fully aware of when, why, and how often they used their screens. Improving their self-awareness would highlight key contributors to their own levels of usage and the after-effects.

Pam and Lee's own relationship with online devices had to change before any kind of positive family outcome could occur. Many of my adult clients experience a massive upheaval in their lives as they go through this process.

Some years ago, I had that problem myself. I know that I experienced the difficulty of being addicted, reaching for my smartphone every couple of minutes to check what I received: Who was it from? What action did I need to take? Did I need to do something immediately? Why was I compelled to do something immediately? For instance, did I need to write a response to a social media post? Or reply to a friend's WhatsApp text, "like" someone's Facebook, Instagram, LinkedIn or Twitter post? The ridiculous anxiety-filled pressure I felt to *have* to respond within a certain time frame was ludicrous. So often, I felt that I had to be really careful with what words I used, the tone, the emojis – was it too much, too little, too friendly, not friendly enough?

As I look back at it now, I realise it didn't make any sense. However, when I was in that situation, I found it completely normal, and I felt that I had to deliver a response … a like, a thumbs up, a smiley face, a sad emoji, a crying emoji, a laughing emoji, some words of wisdom, a congratulatory message to somebody who was having a work anniversary having been at a job for the past six years! On the surface it seems so benign, but something deep inside makes us feel that we need to show up, react and be part of these interactions, which don't really mean very much at all.

I was deeply rooted in that space until I realised it was harming my life; taking over my life. It was overwhelming and took up all my free time. Instead of spending that free time as quality time with my kids, or my wife, or my extended family and friends, I ended up playing Candy Crush, or scrolling through Facebook, or watching endless YouTube videos.

It's time that I will never get back! After each of those multi-hour sessions I spent surfing, viewing other people's highlights – most of which were staged – I would get annoyed with myself for wasting so much time. It would also leave me frustrated, resentful, feeling empty.

Pictures 1, 2 & 3 – Munur's Candy Crush Saga Game on iPhone

Pause for Reflection

What do you notice when you finally break away from a doomscrolling session?

How many times have you taken multiple pictures and posted them on your social media accounts so that it looks like you're having an amazing and wonderful time, but behind the scenes things are very different?

Sometimes our social media presence is very far away from the truth, but how many people post to say they're having a rubbish day, or they feel really stressed by their insurance bill that came in £300 more than it should have been for their car, or somebody upset them at work today, or they're feeling unwell and low, and could really do with a kind and uplifting word or two?

What if we actually told the truth? How would you feel if others saw "beneath your beautiful"?[5]

Do we always have to post positive highlights and experiences to our network? Is life always rosy? Why can't we post something like, "I can't stand having to tell my kids to get off the PlayStation and it's causing me serious aggravation, and their stroppiness, aggressiveness, negativity, and their anger that spills over into my day is driving me insane?"

Posting happy events is not a problem, in itself. It could be a problem if the user is taken away from their social interaction to upload the post. Or for the viewer, if they forget that these are only "highlights" and start to feel like their own life cannot compare with the perceived happiness and achievement portrayed in those pictures and stories.

After some self-examination, Pam and Lee identified their strongest and most prevalent reasons for being online, which apps they used most, why and how they used them. We then looked at the underlying reasons and what they could do to change how they used those apps. At the same time we looked at why they felt the way they felt, and if there was something else that they could be doing. Could they be using their time more effectively? Who would they spend that time with? How could they use that time more positively?

Both Pam and Lee noticed a strong need to be online so that they could be available to respond, fuelled by a belief that if they went off-line they'd miss out on "everything" their friends and family were doing. I challenged those beliefs with the following question: "What would be the impact to you if you didn't go online and see the highlights of your friends and family – what difference would it make to your day-to-day life?" They both gave similar answers in that they would feel free and have time for so much more in their lives.

While collaborating with me in these sessions Pam and Lee replaced old anchors that would have triggered the urge to be online with new emotional responses and experiences. It was also an opportunity to reevaluate their priorities and entertain new possibilities for how they wanted to move forward in their lives as a family. They realised how much more time they could spend with each other, and quality time that they could spend with their kids.

We looked at new experiences that they could create with their children – play games, explore the outdoors, go for bike rides, take them swimming, go to the park, meet with friends and their children. All this screen-free time meant that they would be able to experience real life, thus dampening down the residual effects of the online world.

We agreed to reduce the amount of time that their children were allowed to be on any screen, which meant physically removing screens from their sight. Within a month their home could become a screen-free environment! The kids would be allowed to use screens on special occasions. This would be carefully monitored, and it would be within the confines of specific environments. They would only be allowed on a screen for a limited time with their parents alongside them, which was a crucial step and a massive change from their once "normal" routine. It would be *the* step which started to change the relationship with screens for Pam and Lee's children.

Stage 2 – No Screen Policy

Pam and Lee were determined in their implementation of the second stage of the strategy. They completely removed all screens, all the time, from their children's eyesight, whatever the circumstances. This was more difficult and involved a lot more interaction between Pam, Lee and their children. It also meant that they had to be crystal clear that no screens were visible when visiting with their friends and extended family.

It took time for Pam and Lee to get used to using their screens separately from their children. The children needed to be completely shielded so that they had no idea that Pam and Lee were using screens. From the children's perspective, it had to become a screen-free house, primarily to eliminate Kate's dangerous and destructive behaviour, and also to create a brand-new reality for their son.

Stage 3 – Weekly Plans

Stage three involved Pam and Lee creating a detailed plan on a week-by-week basis. It determined how they would interact, which one of them would be available, when and what activities they would introduce to their kids and be part of. This was an incredibly important part of the strategy and is something that Jonathan Haidt alluded to in his book *The Anxious Generation*[1] – the idea that we make a conscious choice to return to a phone-free or digital-free, play-based childhood.

This encourages our children to learn and interact with other children and with their parents, to learn and enjoy new experiences, being unafraid to try new things. This enables them to create long-lasting memories and new abilities, and the confidence to build upon them over time. A play-based childhood is vital for our children's overall growth – physically, mentally, emotionally and spiritually.

The fundamental learning from this case points directly to the way we choose to parent our children; the crux of it being how we spend our time with our children, ensuring it is quality time. This means making our interactions with them interesting and fun, both co-operative and competitive, intriguing, and most of all exploratory. Our children need to explore – they need to take risks, because this is how they learn, this is how their brain, with specific attention to their prefrontal cortex, grows.

Make every attempt possible to reduce your time spent looking at screens. The brain absorbs the constant stream of instantaneous dopamine hits when gaming and viewing social media. It develops into a craving, which needs ever-greater gratification – more extreme online experiences to create the same level of excitement, thereby fuelling an ever-increasing need for dopamine spikes. This is how our behaviour is systematically altered and how we get hooked! That is where the addiction happens; that is the downfall for our children and us adults.

Pam and Lee's detailed plans, once agreed, would need to be followed through if they were to improve their family wellbeing. They had to keep following those plans of interaction with their children – for instance, playing card games or Lego, kicking a ball, dancing, reading, or trying any other sports and activities. Pam and Lee embraced the new plan as part of this inspiring progressive change in their lives, to ensure the complete break-up with the online world for their kids, and a renewed relationship with tech for themselves. As they worked through the detailed weekly plans, the new activities became second nature, eventually becoming a normal part of their lives.

Conclusion

By taking drastic and disciplined personal positive action, Pam and Lee changed the course of their lives and their children's lives. They succeeded in overhauling screen time for the entire family.

The impact on Kate was phenomenal. Her behaviour towards her young brother changed completely. She became more caring, more empathetic, more relaxed, and in fact a lot more fun, happy and adventurous. Kate started suggesting playing games with her brother which were mainly outdoors and involved having fun in the garden, creating obstacle courses with outdoor furniture and playthings, playing with a ball, and playing with their sand pit, to mention a few. This would have been unheard of a few months earlier.

The children embraced more risky activities like riding scooters and tricycles and learning to ride a bike. Prior to this, they had shown no interest in doing these types of things. But they were now taking part in healthy outdoor activities with great excitement. Kate's behaviour at school also changed. Her teachers reported that she was helping other children, being interactive, kind, calm, inquisitive and, above all, happy and a pleasure to have around.

The most satisfying thing was seeing the incredible positive impact on Kate. Since the removal of screens, Kate had not once deliberately hurt her brother. For Pam and Lee this was just like winning the lottery … it was a dream come true. It was something they couldn't have believed would be possible six months earlier.

As for Kate and Lee's son, Toby, he started to mirror, match and learn and was a much happier toddler. All he wanted to do was play outside with his older sister. Whenever they could, Pam and Lee would interact with the children – they would sit and play with them whether that was indoors or outdoors. They would encourage play dates with friends from Toby's nursery or play group and Kate's school, and they would ensure that all the children interacted with one another and that there wasn't a single screen in sight; it was a complete change-around!

There was a win for Pam and Lee too. Their lives and relationship with each other had an extremely positive fundamental shift, which created an openness, understanding, and ability to be honest with each other without judgement or criticism, which enhanced the lives of the entire family.

In creating a safe space Pam and Lee were able to actively listen to each other and not judge or confront in an aggressive fashion. They created a happy togetherness in their relationship which was constantly highlighted by their friends and family. They worked hard at this and successfully turned around the deeply unpleasant situation the family had found itself in earlier.

Six months on, Pam, Lee, Kate and Toby were completely changed people. Their family life was entirely different from the time when I first received that text from Pam.

This doesn't mean that they had become complacent and believed they had the winning formula. They had to keep working at this, as new challenges would arise, and screens would naturally come to play a part in their family lives as the children's needs changed. Screens would be re-introduced in a balanced tech-aware household with boundaries and rules fully in place.

What I want to stress here is that screens can have a positive role and can add value if they are used appropriately – if they are used with knowledge, awareness, care, and empathy.

Pam and Lee are dynamic and moving forward on a positive journey, encouraging their children to grow with a play-based childhood and not a screen-based childhood. We continue to meet monthly to discuss where they are, what they've done, what the ups and downs are, and what they can implement to keep up the positive change they have created.

Initially, Lee was very much against Pam reaching out for help. However, he has done a 180-degree turn and has told me the intervention brought a complete and positive transformation in his life!

Both he and Pam wanted others to know about their story, and that with help, with deep and extensive and sometimes uncomfortable change, their family life and relationships were completely turned around.

If you would like to know more about becoming a parent-coach, scan the QR code below for the Rebel Insights page at www.RebelTherapies.com where you can find various downloadable information sheets and top tips which are mentioned in this book.

Chapter 5

Good Nude Bad Nude

To send a nude photo or not to send a nude photo – that is the question.

What's behind the desire for a person to send a nude photograph to a complete stranger? Why would anyone want to send a picture of their most intimate and private parts to a person they don't know and have never met? In many cases they are not sending it to the person they think they're sending it to – it's actually being sent to a business that extorts vast sums of money from vulnerable people. This has become a serious global issue affecting tens of thousands of people, and if handled badly can cause the person sending the nude photographs extreme distress.

In this case study things really got out of control, to the point where a teenager was so distressed that his parents were concerned he might take his own life. It was at this point when his father reached out to me for help.

I would normally refer the parent to their local GP, charities like the Samaritans, Mind and Childline, or a psychologist to get emergency help from experts who have the right skills to deal with someone in this delicate situation.

However, this was slightly different, and I had to act immediately to help this distraught father and son.

When his father, Jamal, called and asked for my intervention, he gave me a detailed explanation of Samir's story and the situation as it currently stood.

It Was All Great Until It Wasn't!

Samir had become friendly with two young girls, also teenagers, via his Snapchat account. Samir was 15 and both girls were 14 at the time. Samir lived with his family in Slough, and the two girls lived in Glasgow.

The girls found Samir via his profile on Snapchat and had reached out and connected with him. They had formed a relationship over the space of three months.

Samir engaged with the girls in a series of messages which became very sexually explicit. The two girls were best friends and were looking to have some fun online, just as other teenagers do. This seems to be a normal part of life for teens in this day and age – a far cry from what life was like when I was a teenager in the 1990s.

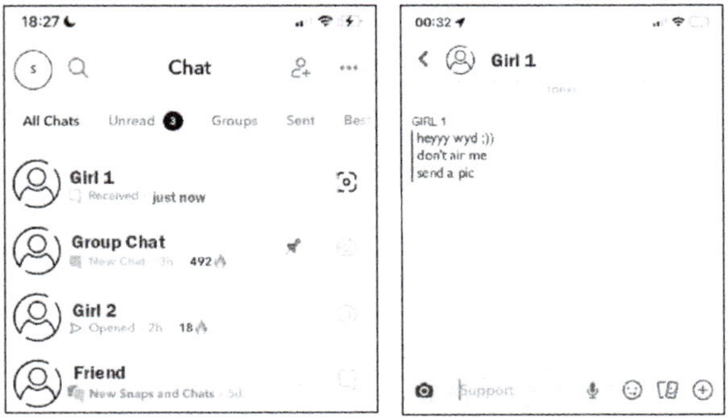

Pictures 1 & 2. Snapchat Example

Samir on the other hand was new to this type of interaction on social media. He went to an all-boys school and was very inexperienced in terms of relationships with girls. In fact, he had never had a girlfriend, and he had never experienced the type of attention that he was receiving from these two girls.

In just three months, Samir and the girls exchanged more than 600 messages, which included multiple naked photos. I found out that the girls had sent about 80 to 100 photos of themselves, individually, together, and some where they performed different sex acts on each other. They also sent him lots of voice messages as well as at least 10 very explicit videos.

This was quite an eye-opening experience for Samir and made him feel extremely privileged but, more so, excited about the thought of getting into some sort of physical sexual relationship with these two girls.

There was, however, an imbalance in the relationship between Samir and the two girls which caused serious problems to unfold in the months ahead. Samir wasn't as comfortable or as forthcoming as the girls when it came to sending naked pictures back to them. In fact, over the three months of their online "relationship", he sent only three specific photos of himself, one of which was a "dick-pic" (a picture of his penis). However, this didn't appease the two girls.

During those three months the girls had bombarded Samir with pictures, enticing him to reciprocate by sending similarly explicit pictures and videos of himself.

When Samir refused to send the girls a video performing a sex act on himself, the girls turned nasty. They threatened that they would send the pictures of him to all their friends and to Samir's friendship group, as the girls had managed to link in with a significant number of Samir's friends.

The girls were furious that Samir would not comply with their wishes and wanted to teach him a lesson, so they did a couple of things. Firstly, they went ahead with their threats and sent the pictures to their whole network, which included Samir's friends. However, that wasn't enough for these girls, as they wanted to really hurt him. They told their parents that Samir had aggressively threatened them over the course of their interaction; that they'd felt bullied and pressurised into sending the pictures and videos to Samir. They told their parents Samir had threatened to kill them if they didn't comply with his demands.

All of this was a complete lie and a gross misrepresentation of what had really happened, but it was enough to persuade the girls' parents to call the police. They reported Samir to the police and said he was part of a grooming team that were trying to entice the girls and get them into prostitution. The situation escalated very quickly because of the problems which have been highlighted in the news in recent years, regarding the activity of grooming groups in the northwest of England. The police took the girls' complaint very seriously and contacted their counterparts in Slough.

The first time that Jamal heard about this – even though he had noticed substantial changes in his son's behaviour and mood in the house – was when he had a knock at the door late one afternoon, and in front of him were four burly policemen. Without any real discussion they mentioned they had a very serious complaint by underage minors who had accused Samir of being part of a nationwide grooming gang. They wanted to take him in for questioning.

Jamal said that he went into complete shock and kept telling the officers there must have been some mistake. He told me that the police refused to answer any of Jamal's questions and insisted on taking Samir to the police station for questioning.

Jamal talked me through that exact moment, explaining that his heart sank, and he was overwhelmed by shock, stress and confusion at the turn of events. He also had no idea what he could or should do from a legal standpoint. Samir was taken to the police station with his father, and what happened next was just unbelievable. The police utterly failed to do their job properly – they questioned Samir as though he was guilty. Not once did they stop to ask Samir his side of the story. The police said they would be pressing charges, they had evidence of links between Samir and grooming gangs in the Midlands, this would lead to a "very serious court hearing", and that the consequences for Samir would be disastrous.

Jamal told me he had suspected Samir was up to something, but did not realise it was quite as serious as this.

Samir was a typical teenager, spending nearly all of his free time on his smartphone or his iPad, locked away in his room either gaming or on YouTube or other social media late at night. The addictive effects of these technologies are so powerful that adolescents are developmentally ill-equipped to navigate this tech in a rational, moderated and balanced way.

Support for Samir

My initial advice to Jamal was to get a lawyer as soon as possible as this would definitely go to court. I advised Jamal to download and take screenshots of all the images and videos, if Samir still had them, as well as all the texts – every bit of correspondence with the girls. This was to ensure Samir's defence would be able to back up their argument that it was in fact Samir who was the one being bullied and harassed by these two girls.

The next suggestion was to get Samir to see a child psychologist to receive some immediate help for his emotional and mental state, because dealing with something like this is incredibly distressing. Jamal didn't want to wait until the morning and asked me to speak with his son immediately. He was concerned that his son had completely withdrawn, falling into a severe downward spiral, and he was extremely worried for Samir's physical wellbeing. Jamal was terrified that Samir would do something life-threatening to himself.

Jamal's call had come very late in the evening and, at first, I didn't answer. He then texted me saying he was a friend of a friend and really needed my help immediately. Jamal reached out again and this time I answered. Our conversation went on for well over an hour, and then I spoke directly to Samir.

My conversation with Samir was about creating a safe space to express himself without any judgement, and actively listening while he explained how he felt about what was happening.

I asked Samir to explain his version of events and what he was feeling at that particular moment. He was distraught; he couldn't believe this was happening to him. He felt deeply ashamed of himself and embarrassed to face his family. Samir talked for quite a while, and I just listened, occasionally asking him questions with no judgement, allowing him to just talk through what he was feeling.

What was important at this moment was that I offer no real advice or ask him why and how he got himself in this situation in the first place – none of that mattered! What was important was to make him feel heard, not judged, just simply understood; that he was in a safe space and could say whatever he wanted.

As we talked, I used some coaching and NLP (Neuro-Linguistic Programming) techniques to diffuse the anxiety Samir was feeling. I explained that although this was an incredibly stressful time for Samir, and even though he was feeling terribly ashamed by the situation – "stress" and "shame" were the two main words that Samir constantly used – he had a loving family supporting him and that he wasn't alone.

This type of experience happens to many others up and down the country, and throughout the rest of the world. I told Samir about other situations I'd come across and some of the other teenage boys I had helped over the past few years, who were in similar situations, to let him know that these experiences were not uncommon.

I explained to Samir that he would eventually feel okay about this, and to get to that space we had some work to do together – that there was a process to follow, and that process had different stages. Each stage had its own specific individual steps that had to be carried out. Once I explained the stages and steps of the process to Samir, he completely understood it – he even likened it to playing a game of chess. By implementing the right strategy and stepping through it one chess move at a time, together we would be able to win this very difficult and stressful game that we had been forced to play. I pointed out to Samir that he had the capability to regain control of his life.

At the end of that initial call, Samir told me he felt relieved when he understood that he wasn't the only person this was happening to, and that explaining the situation to his father and then to me had massively reduced his levels of severe desperation, stress, shame and anxiety. He even came up with a novel way of explaining his different levels of stress and anxiety by comparing them to nuclear threat levels.

He mentioned that he had originally been at DEFCON 1. However, after our conversation he was closer to the bottom end of DEFCON 2. I found his explanation really interesting. When I asked him what DEFCON 1 meant to him and what the step after DEFCON 1 would be, he told me that the only thing left after DEFCON 1 *"would be the end"*.

Readiness Condition	Exercise Term	Description	Readiness
DEFCON 1	COCKED PISTOL	Nuclear war is imminent or has already started	Maximum readiness. Immediate response.
DEFCON 2	FAST PACE	Next step to nuclear war	Armed forces ready to deploy and engage in less than six hours
DEFCON 3	ROUND HOUSE	Increase in force readiness above that required for normal readiness	Air Force ready to mobilise in 15 minutes
DEFCON 4	DOUBLE TAKE	Increased intelligence watch and security measures	Above normal readiness
DEFCON 5	FADE OUT	Lowest state of readiness	Normal readiness

Table 1. DEFCON Levels

I chose not to ask him where he was on the DEFCON 1 level, instead concentrating on asking him about moving along the DEFCON levels, and what he could do to move towards DEFCON 5. His immediate response was that in talking with me and knowing his family was supporting him and not judging or angry with him, he was moving in the right direction.

I worked very closely with Samir and Jamal to help the family over the course of six months to get them through this very difficult time.

The Three-Stage Plan

We broke our process down into three stages:

Stage 1 – Immediate Intervention

This immediate intervention meant continuing with a daily discussion with both Samir and Jamal for the first few weeks. The purpose was to get them both to a place where we could normalise what had happened, where Samir didn't feel overwhelmed or judged by his parents, and then to change how he felt and viewed himself. For Jamal, he needed to separate his anger about Samir getting himself into such a ridiculous situation, so he could focus on being compassionate and protective of his son. We also looked at other ways the situation affected Jamal emotionally, mentally and physically. It had an impact on all the family, but the most stressful times were dealing with the police, who Jamal felt should have been less judgemental, more empathetic and more helpful to him and his family.

Stage 2 – The Court Case

Keeping every single piece of evidence possible was one of the most important pieces of advice I gave to Jamal and Samir. They took screenshots of every message and downloaded every image and video that the two girls had sent Samir. They kept every message and any image that Samir had sent back to the two girls. Their evidence formed the basis of the court case and ensured that the right decision was made.

Stage 3 – A New Beginning
This stage dealt with the fallout from the court case which helped to forge a new beginning for Samir and his family. This meant establishing new positive anchors for everything that related to engaging with technology; creating depth, strength and honesty in their internal relationships as a family; and creating a safe environment where Samir could look towards creating healthy relationships with the opposite sex in the future.

Before we look at the details of each stage, I want to describe a conversation I had with Samir during this time about the reasons he got involved with these two girls.

Samir's Naivety

Samir mentioned that from the age of 11 he had very little opportunity to interact with girls because he went to an all-boys grammar school. His school life was so intense that he rarely had any free time outside of schoolwork, school clubs, or social activities directly linked to his school. For years he could count on one hand how many times he had any kind of conversation with a girl of a similar age to himself.

Before secondary school, Samir had gone to a mixed-sex nursery and primary school. He also had a younger sister, so he was used to playing with girls and mixing freely with them. Interacting with girls was never really an issue prior to him going to secondary school.

This is something that happens quite often – I've encountered several cases in my work where, as young boys turn into teens and go through puberty, there is a disconnect with how they navigate their feelings and any interaction with the opposite sex.

Samir mentioned that as he grew up and moved through the stages of puberty and early adolescence, he felt more and more isolated from the opposite sex. He felt most awkward when in the company of a girl of a similar age, especially if he had to go to a family event or a party or other social situation. In my experience, that level of awkwardness is not unusual. High levels of anxiety, desperation, shame and the fear of failure cause teens to have real difficulty interacting.

For a teenage boy like Samir, the need to feel wanted, to have a girl interested in him specifically, is paramount. Not having had any kind of relationship or intimacy with a girl at his age made him feel worthless, embarrassed and stressed. He mentioned that the boys at his school were always bragging about the relationships that they were having with girls, saying "they've had sex already". They also talked about their multiple online interactions with different girls, and viewing porn sites like Pornhub and OnlyFans. For young male teens, this all comes with the territory and is laced with a heavy dose of pressure to conform and perform! Samir felt this incessant pressure to prove himself to his friends and to himself, to show that he was equal to them.

The pressure to fit in is unbelievably high for this Gen Z generation, especially as it relates to their standing in their peer group in the online space. The feedback I often receive from this age group is that it suffocates their sense of freedom. It is something that we parents have not yet fully grasped, because not many adults over 30 had this sort of experience when growing up.

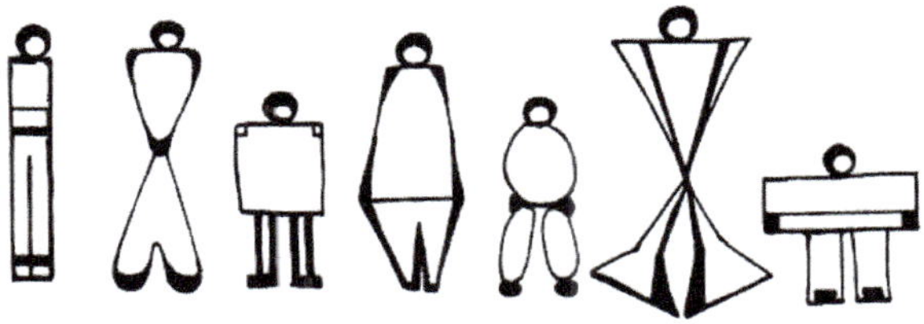

Picture 3. Perfect Body Shapes

This pressure should not be underestimated and comes in many forms. For some it is having the "perfect" body shape, for others it is the plumpness of their lips, the shape of their eyes, or the contours of their cheekbones. This pressure often comes from well-paid influencers, or from misogynistic icons like Andrew Tate.

His rhetoric is poisonous to the young immature adolescent minds of boys and is causing skewed ideas about how boys relate to girls.

Samir explained that to fit in he had to subscribe to certain channels and groups, like Andrew Tate's. It didn't matter if he liked or agreed with the images or ideas promoted on these sites, he just needed to fit in. His fear of being cast aside and missing out (FoMO)[1] outweighed anything else. The desperate urge to feel part of a group and to feel accepted means that our Gen Z generation are conforming to unhealthy peer group norms, even if it is against every fibre of their being, because of the strength and depth of power wielded by the dopamine-saturated online social Wild West.

Many adults I have spoken to in recent years don't really understand their children's burning desire for acceptance by their peers online or the pressure they feel to compromise their values and beliefs in order to fit in.

If we are to help our adolescents through the confusion of their growing pains during puberty, we need to be more open, empathetic and non-judgemental in our exchanges with them. We need to listen carefully, and not react by blaming our children for their actions, thoughts and words. We need to carefully create an open and safe environment full of love, care, compassion and freedom of expression to support and even prevent other young people getting into situations similar to Samir's.

Since my in-depth conversations with Samir, he felt like he was in a much more resilient and sustainable space. Once we had identified and talked about the very fickle and flaky peer groups that Samir was part of, he was able to navigate the online world and social media in a much healthier way. He realised that many of his friends were posting messages, images and ideas in those groups which were not real – they were made-up!

What also became apparent was that even though Samir was desperate to have some sort of experience with a girl, he was only doing this because of the pressure from his friends. He told me he didn't mind not having a relationship or a girlfriend until he was ready. Samir came to this conclusion on his own after our discussions. It was then that he realised he wasn't ready, and he was only doing this because of how the non-truths that his friends were posting on their chats made him feel.

Samir's insights helped create a healthier and far more open family environment. After going through this very painful experience, he was stronger, more capable, and had a deeper understanding of who he was. Samir deleted all but one social media channel, keeping just WhatsApp for his school and family groups.

Intervention, Resilience and Change

As mentioned earlier in this chapter, we worked together to create an ecosystem to support and encourage positive change in Samir's life and that of his family in three specific stages.

Stage 1 – Immediate Intervention

The purpose of Stage 1 was to create the platform upon which we could help Samir to rebuild.

The first part of that rebuild was doing the legwork to clear Samir's name, which started with the collation of data. Samir and Jamal downloaded all evidence of any interaction between Samir and the girls. They took screenshots and forwarded all the messages and emailed all the evidence to his father so that they had the complete account of what was happening between Samir and the girls.

The evidence was put into chronological order. Samir was involved in each step to understand and empower him in this process, which would help him get through this part of his journey. All the data was sent to Samir's lawyer as part of the very strong evidence of his innocence.

As part of this stage, I worked closely with Jamal and Samir to ensure we had honest, open and complete lines of communication. This meant daily 1-2-1 discussions between the three of us. These meetings could last anywhere between five minutes and an hour and Samir could discuss anything he wanted. These sessions were to allow Samir to vent his anger, and express his frustrations about anything and anyone, whether it was a teacher, another student, his mother, or the bus driver on the way to school, or about his football team not winning that weekend ... about absolutely anything.

What was important was that Jamal and I would be there to actually listen and allow Samir to express his feelings and thoughts – not to judge or confront him, but just understand him. This new pathway of communication strengthened and deepened Jamal and Samir's relationship and they achieved a level of honesty and trust which previously hadn't existed.

I coached Jamal through this period and taught him some techniques which he could use in his relationships with Samir and other family members.

Through Samir, we introduced the concept of active listening to the entire family unit, including Samir's mother and younger sister. They effectively learnt the art of active listening, becoming non-judgemental and non-confrontational, creating a healthy and safe space to express themselves and talk honestly and openly. This took us through to Stage 2.

Stage 2 – The Court Case

The collection of all the evidence required for the court case was triggering. During this process I worked with the family to desensitise the experience by using some NLP techniques, making it devoid of any real emotion – it became something plain and clinical.

We made it more transactional, a matter of methodically filling out forms and sending information, without investing any emotion in the process, so that they could breathe, feel more relaxed. Removing the emotion and life from this terrible situation – which Jamal called a "beast" – enabled them to get on top of things and create a new narrative for themselves. It empowered them to get through the ordeal.

We worked through their experiences and emotions by understanding their frustration and anger towards different aspects. The three main parties we identified and reframed were:

1. The two teenage girls – why they caused this to happen.
2. The girls' parents – their knee-jerk reaction.
3. The police – they didn't do their job in a professional, fair, caring and empathetic manner.

Samir and his family found strength and support from the school and from their close friends. It was interesting to see that as time went by and after weeks of discussing the case with their lawyers, Jamal and Samir and the rest of the family became more relaxed. They realised they weren't the only ones going through a situation like this as there had been other cases like theirs. They felt more confident and knew that they were in a very strong position to prove Samir had done nothing wrong.

He had not bullied, pressurised or threatened the girls into sending any of the content. He just engaged quite innocently and obviously loved the attention. He would never have agreed to the girls' ultimatum to send videos and explicit pictures of himself to them, and that was a positive strength. I saw that from the very beginning of our interactions and showed Samir that this positive strength would play out in his favour in this whole process.

The courts sided with Samir, and he was completely vindicated. They agreed that the girls had wanted to try and hurt Samir as much as they could. The girls confessed that they wanted to get their way, and when this didn't happen they tried everything they could to cause harm. This all became quite evident in the very short court case. The court also criticised the handling of the case, especially by the police, and made it clear that it should have never reached the courts. The police were criticised for every aspect of the way they handled the case.

The most important outcome here was that Samir felt his voice was heard, and his family's voices were heard regarding the police and their mistreatment of the case. Samir was ecstatic and relieved, and mentioned he couldn't wait to move past this. He and his family could now put it behind them.

Stage 3 – A New Beginning

Our third stage was spent working to create new anchors to embark on a fresh new period in their lives. During this process Samir reflected on his experiences and was able to forge a more sustainable relationship with the digital world.

Conclusion

Cyber bullying comes in many different forms, and it impacts individuals and families in a variety of ways.

In times of need, it can be easy to feel isolated, closed off from the people who are there for us, if we are too ashamed of our actions to reach out for help. We all make mistakes, crave attention, need love and a sense of belonging. It's nice to feel needed, attractive and wanted in various ways. Sometimes we do things that we regret, but those things shouldn't define us or be allowed to harm us through others' actions against us.

It is important that we feel we can trust those around us, and for the people who are closest to us to be non-confrontational and non-judgemental. This allows us to express and discuss things that are very personal without feeling scared, anxious, nervous or that we will be judged in a negative way.

By creating an environment of trust, kindness, empathy, careful and open active listening, we can create dialogue within our family and friendships, to enable our children to feel that they can be honest and be treated in a way that makes them feel loved and safe.

Rebel Insights Tips – Help Protect from Extortion and Blackmail

1. Make sure that all your social media channels are set to private.
2. Make sure to block and /or ignore any connections from strangers.
3. Do not move to a different social media platform if asked by someone you don't know.
4. Do not start a video chat with anyone you don't know.
5. A photo or a video of a new connection who you don't know is not proof that they are who they say they are; this could be an avatar and a front for an organisation looking to extort money from you.
6. Do not send any photos or videos of yourself in any form that could compromise you.
7. Do not send any nude photographs or videos of yourself to anyone, EVER!
8. If anyone is trying to extort money from you, please report this to a loved one, to the police, and to the platform you use to communicate with this person.
9. Keep all evidence. DO NOT DELETE! Make sure you download all messages, pictures, video, and any other interaction so that it can be used by law enforcement.
10. Any image of you that has been uploaded can be removed by request to the following organisation: **The Internet Watch Foundation**, a UK charity set up to help remove sexual images and videos of under 18s posted online:

www.iwf.org.uk/our-technology/report-remove/

11. Please remember that as embarrassing or frightening, stressful or devastating as this may be, you're not the only ones that this is happening to. You are not alone, it happens to many other people, and there is always a solution, a way out to something that is more positive.
12. Parents – stay strong, be resilient, and create an open, safe and caring environment for your children to converse.
13. Adopt active listening skills. Never aggressively confront and never judge, just be fully present with empathy, care, love and kindness.

If you would like to know more about becoming a parent-coach, scan the QR code below for the Rebel Insights page at www.RebelTherapies.com where you can find various downloadable information sheets and top tips which are mentioned in this book.

Chapter 6

Lockdown Shutdown!

Reluctance to go to school is not a new phenomenon – it's probably existed as long as schools have. There have always been children who really don't want to go to school, for a variety of reasons. It could be that they just do not like it, or have anxiety and stress about making new friends, creating relationships and interacting in a setting that they don't feel comfortable with. However, school refusal has become more common since the use of smartphones really took hold in around 2012 when front facing cameras were popularised[1]. The advancement of technology and the resulting ability to lose ourselves in screens, combined with the endless amount of information we can access in the online world, has made it easier for our children to push back on going to school.

The issue of children being reluctant or refusing to go to school became a crisis after the first COVID-19 lockdown in March 2020. The levels of anxiety increased dramatically for many people, but none more so than our children. Nearly everything we did went online, and we were forced to remain in our family units, unable to interact socially in the physical environment that we were used to – and I believe we need as human beings.

This phenomenon, sometimes called "school phobia" or "school anxiety"[2] has meant that numerous parents and carers have found themselves in very difficult situations trying to navigate their children's refusal to go to school alongside the struggles of day-to-day life.

Some of the reasons why a child refuses to go to school are illustrated in this case study, alongside other difficulties faced by a young teenager, Amy, and her parents.

Amy's Anxiety

When I was asked to help Amy in 2022 she was 14. Amy's problems first became apparent late in 2019 when she was 11, a year before the COVID pandemic. Prior to this, Amy came across as a happy child, was always in a group of friends, and never seemed like the type of person who would prefer to be alone. She had a best friend and generally went to school willingly, even though she never really loved it.

As Year 9 progressed, Amy started to show signs of withdrawal from nearly everything. When she came home from school she would not interact as much as she used to, and she would head upstairs to her bedroom and lock herself in her room saying that she was doing homework.

It was at this point that Amy started to spend more time endlessly doomscrolling and watching hours and hours of videos on YouTube, Instagram and TikTok. This took over her life and the effect of what she was hearing, seeing and feeling through these videos and "reels" completely altered her behaviour. Amy turned from a confident teenager to a quivering wreck, constantly comparing her physical appearance with the influencers' "perfect bodies". Amy's father, Max, noticed the change in her personality. He became concerned about her withdrawal from "normal life" into a screen-based world dominated by social media and all the messages it gave her about what she "should" look like.

This behaviour persisted for months. The situation got worse over time. When Amy came home there would be less and less interaction with her parents and siblings and she would only make an appearance for dinner, then return to her room. As this continued, Amy started to show odd behaviour relating to hygiene – she wouldn't let anyone into her room and would not go anywhere without hand sanitiser.

As the situation evolved Amy would tell her parents most mornings that she felt unwell and couldn't go to school. On some occasions, Amy would deliberately throw up, although her parents were initially unaware that she did so on purpose.

Amy's mum, Sandra, contacted me in the spring of 2022. The situation in the household had become untenable because of the effort required to manage Amy.

Sandra explained that she was desperately struggling to manage their home life. She had two other children who were younger than Amy, and relationships in her immediate and extended family had been strained by the impact of Amy's situation. This is why Sandra reached out for help.

Amy's decline didn't happen overnight. There was a slow progression and initially they felt they had the experience and skills to be able to manage.

Sandra said that initially they did manage the situation, and it wasn't too difficult to get Amy ready for school. The bigger problem was what happened when she got back from school. There would be a sudden change in her attitude and personality. Over time Amy would hide herself away and avoid interacting with her family more and more. Things then went from not so good to disastrous when COVID broke out. Sandra told me it felt as if they "fell off a cliff".

The mental and physical impact of that first major lockdown in the spring of 2020 was not fully realised until lockdown was lifted. While Sandra and her family were at home during the lockdown it was great. There was an early summer as the weather in April in the UK was glorious. Amy seemed more relaxed and was able to engage with her schoolwork, although her behaviour was not quite the same as it had been pre-September 2019, when she would spend time with the family and be around all the time.

Initially, Sandra put the changes in Amy down to hormones and growing through puberty. However, Amy's behaviour was not normal – it was something more extreme which needed immediate and careful intervention. Later when Amy's parents reflected on this period, they were able to recognise that her condition was more severe than just puberty-related development and far more impactful emotionally, mentally and physically.

It wasn't found out until later on that Amy developed "tunnel vision" in her focus on hygiene. This was a result of watching countless videos about germs and cleaning on YouTube. She insisted that anyone coming into her room had to use hand sanitiser. The use of hand sanitiser was extreme, not the "normal" expected usage. Amy used so much sanitiser that her hands got chemical burns. At the same time Amy's behaviour and personality altered noticeably. Between September 2019 and March 2020 Amy changed from a very happy, gentle, loving daughter who used to regularly hang out with her best friend and do everything with her, to a very isolated, emotionally drained, quiet and withdrawn adolescent.

The fun interactions at home with her siblings and parents after school gradually slowed to a stop over that six-month period. Sandra explained that as Amy moved into Year 10 at school, the first year of GCSEs, her behaviour changed again. There were lots of new things happening and Amy's decisive efforts to avoid school and obtain schoolwork to do at home were making life very difficult for her parents. They faced a real battle to get her dressed and off to school, as she wouldn't allow anybody into her room.

One day in November 2020 Amy decided that she wasn't going to school any more. She barricaded herself in her room, only leaving to make quick dashes to the bathroom. Sandra mentioned that the only way she could get Amy to eat was to leave a plate of food on a tray outside her room, walk away and then send Amy a text message telling her that her food was outside her door. Only then would Amy open her door, take the tray and once finished leave the tray outside. Sandra remarked sarcastically that it was a bit like room service but in her own home. She suddenly realised that their relationship with their daughter had broken down. They were at tipping point.

Another aspect to this immensely delicate and difficult situation was the swing in her hygiene choice. When Amy's use of hand sanitiser became so obsessive that the skin on her hands burned, her parents had to forcibly removed it from her.

While this stopped Amy burning her hands, it also had consequences that Sarah and Max couldn't have foreseen. Instead of her super clean rituals, Amy swung in the complete opposite direction. She ceased to care about cleanliness and would refuse to wash.

Sandra mentioned that there were times when Amy went weeks without having a shower, or wash, or allowing her mum to help her in any way towards her hygiene.

Sandra and Max were constantly in touch with the school and the Social Services Department to update them on the situation. However, no one could or would do anything to assist with changing Amy's behaviour. It took a lot of courage and numerous internal discussions with Max and extended family for Sandra to forge some sort of change.

Intervention

I started working with Sandra and Max to see what strategies we could put in place to initiate change in their household. They were really struggling at this point, and their two younger children had also begun complaining about going to school. They were old enough to be able to demand, "If Amy can stay at home, then why can't we?"

Amy had a few elements in her life that contributed to her current state. However, the most significant catalyst was COVID. As a society we were impacted in many ways by the pandemic and we won't understand the true cost of its effect for years. But I believe the greatest cost of COVID was the mental, emotional and physical toll on young people.

When I first started working with Sandra and Max, I spent time exploring their family dynamic – what it looked like before the noticeable changes to Amy, then during COVID, and after all the lockdowns and restrictions were lifted. I needed to understand everything they did in their family unit to piece together how they got to their current state. In doing so, we could start implementing carefully constructed strategies, and I could teach them some Jedi mind tricks to elicit positive change.

The fallout from Amy not going to school spread into many different areas of their lives. Sandra's two younger children were impacted by Amy's withdrawal from general home life as their relationship with their older sister stopped completely. That kind of relationship change in any household is difficult for the parents, not to mention the impact it has on the siblings.

Sandra explained that they had to create a new normal in their household. They would have to do activities with the younger children without Amy present. Sandra and Max were too scared to leave Amy alone in the house because they didn't know what might happen. Ensuring that there would always be an adult in the house caused incredible stress and frustration between Sandra and Max. There was also a great deal of tension between Sandra and her parents, and Max and his parents.

In situations like these there can be a knee-jerk reaction to pin the blame on someone, and that usually takes the form of one parent blaming the other, or the grandparents blaming the parents for not parenting "properly". In some instances, the way parents react from the outset creates what comes next. If, as a parent, you stand back and allow your child to dictate and to create their own narrative, things can go bad very quickly. There is a very delicate balance between being a friend, being kind and being a parent. If that balance is upset problems inevitably arise.

Boundaries are very important for children and teens as they grow. If we don't put them in place from the outset, and course correct according to the age and maturity of our children, we can open ourselves up to disruption, disobedience, destruction and even anarchy.

Parents need to ensure there are suitable ground rules for children to navigate and learn what is and isn't acceptable. We cannot allow our children to find their way without some guidance – without some care, responsibility and consideration on our part.

There are going to be ups and downs, challenges and changes in behaviour and emotions as children grow through puberty and adolescence to become young adults. As they go through this process it is essential that they find their own way, make mistakes and solve problems, within the bounds of a healthy, constructive, fulfilling and risk-taking lifestyle.

Sandra and Max did not take steps to agree an approach to course correct and assert timely boundaries in the early stages when Amy's problems began. Unsure of the underlying reasons for Amy's disturbing behaviour, they hoped things would return to normal on their own. By not deciding a strategy to communicate what behaviour was and wasn't reasonable they gave free rein to their child to create new rules and behaviours, which were detrimental to the family ecosystem.

Each parent told me they avoided dealing with the situation because they thought it was just a phase Amy was going through, and "it was just her being a stroppy teenager". Because they did not lay down some clear and defined boundaries, Amy spiralled downwards, and it became much harder to steer her back to a positive space.

Sandra and Max had trouble recognising the severity of the problem because COVID was so destructive for them from a social interactive perspective and their current state of affairs became deep-rooted. To tackle the problem head-on they decided, after numerous conversations with friends and family, to take concrete action and reach for an intervention.

By the time Sandra approached me, Amy was already nearly two years down the track in creating her own isolated world. Amy's world shrank to the confines of the four walls of her bedroom. She had not been out of the house for nearly two years other than to go to the doctor due to ill health, and on a couple of occasions to school, after being forced by her father. Amy spent nearly 700 days at home.

Amy lost touch with her friends. She completely stopped communicating with her best friend. Her schoolwork suffered, her hygiene and physical health suffered, and her mental and emotional stability hit rock bottom.

This is not an uncommon issue. Unfortunately, levels of stress and anxiety increase exponentially when the same cycle is repeated again and again, which was so obviously observed in Amy's case. An example of this is if your child doesn't go to school on the Monday because they say they are unwell, and if they stay in the comfort of their own home with technology like smartphones and iPads at their fingertips, there is no chance to get bored, so there's less incentive to go in the next day. Added to this is the worry about the work that needs to be caught up from the missed lessons. With all this in mind, the child calls in sick again the next day, and the vicious cycle begins. Stress and anxiety build up, as does the missed schoolwork. If this is left unchecked, and if the right levers aren't pulled at the right times by parents and the school, to provide support and ensure the child can handle the pressure, a relatively manageable situation turns into a minefield of problems.

As this escalates, the child's mental and emotional state worsens – commonly because they are worrying so much about what others are thinking and saying about them.

These projections can cause distress and paranoia; their emotionally charged beliefs are running amok. There is a tendency for the child to believe they're being identified as a problem and rumours are being spread about them in the online community within their school and their friendship groups. Their minds create the perception that "everybody is talking about" them and their problems.

In some cases, through their actions, children in this situation do actually become the focal point of gossip and rumours, and this fuels online bullying. This has multiple implications, especially if the child views this content alone in their bedroom, which should be their safe haven. The safe space shatters like broken glass as it is invaded by their peer groups in the online world.

The online world is a space where comments and pictures can have a massive reach. Online bullying doesn't take place in a one-to-one environment. The reach of these messages is one-to-many. This means that if somebody writes something it's usually in a chat group, and therefore goes out to many people within that person's social media landscape and can go viral. A child's social standing in the online world can be destroyed by a simple message – a non-truth that becomes "real and true", validated by the number of times it's shared and viewed.

In Amy's case some of these negative things did happen. The online bullying started to gain momentum at the same time Amy's fear of COVID took hold. The idea of carrying COVID from school into her home, or passing it on to her grandparents, and the implications of that in her confused mind, created an overload in her own mental capacity which was devastating.

There were multiple layers of stress and anxiety for Amy to deal with, some of which she herself had created through her endless ruminating about what others were thinking of her. Then the next layer was the worry about missing her classes, as she was in her first year of GCSEs, and wondering how she could possibly catch up on all the work she was missing.

At the same time Amy was being pressed by her best friend to tell her what was wrong, and why she wasn't going to school. Initially Amy would say she was unwell and had stomach cramps that were so bad she couldn't go to school. However, Amy could only use this excuse for a short period of time. Her friend became more insistent about asking what else was wrong and if there was anything she could do, as she wanted to come round and see Amy.

Amy's situation went from bad to worse and her nightmares came true, as online bullying and rumours began to be spread by kids at school, since she was away for such a long time. The school brought in the social worker team from the council to discuss what was happening with her parents and how they could be of help. Sandra and Max tried to coax Amy out of her room, with the help of one of her teachers and a social worker at different times, but it didn't help. The longer this went on the worse it became for Amy, and she spiralled downward. The whole situation was getting completely out of control.

The levels of online bullying and hate, and the destructive comments that came from some of the groups Amy was part of were so nasty that a deep hatred of anything connected with school grew within her. Self-harming became an issue for Amy at this point.

There were multiple layers here, so we had to approach the situation very carefully and in a staged manner. We split our strategy into three main stages.

Stage 1 – Communication is Key

The first thing we had to do was remove the idea that not going to school was an option for both Amy and her siblings, and establish a clear line of communication that was acceptable for Sandra, Max and Amy. Stage 1 was broken up into three steps:

Step 1 – Role Models

I held a session with Sandra and Max to help me understand how the two younger children were feeling, and to gently put in place steps to encourage them both to go to school. This entailed giving them clear-cut reasons why school was interesting, fun and beneficial to them, and how it would help them in the coming days, weeks and months, and more so how they would be role models for their older sister. This was one of the best drivers for the two younger siblings. They would be able to show Amy how great going to school was, and they loved the idea of being role models for their older sister. They also felt empowered by the idea they were helping Amy out of her horrible situation, and that it could help the family back to a resilient, balanced and sustainable, happy place.

Step 2 – Dialogue

The second step was to create a dialogue between one of the parents and Amy. There had to be a single point of contact for Amy. This task fell to Sandra. It was important to create a trusting and caring line of communication for Amy. Sandra's approach had to be devoid of judgement, anger, frustration or stress. Her role was to just listen, remaining calm and caring so they could start making very small changes to Amy's behaviour.

Step 3 – School Involvement

We wanted to normalise some of what was happening and wanted to get the school involved as early as possible. As we were making these initial changes the school would be involved from the outset and understand what the timeline for the return to school would look like. This meant opening a line of communication between Amy and her favourite teacher. There was no pressure, no stress, and no judgement. It was done by slowly introducing the teacher into the conversations that Amy was having with her mother. As this became normal for Amy, we agreed that her teacher would directly message with Amy, keeping her parents informed about the messages, to ensure that all parties were aligned. It was important that we were in sync with each other every step of the way to help create very small and substantial change for Amy over time. It took months to create that trust, confidence, and honesty between Amy and her family, and then between Amy and her teachers.

Stage 2 – Family Re-Integration

The aim of this stage was to increase the level of interaction and conversation between Amy and her mother, and slowly include her father Max. Another part of this was to incorporate Amy into the family dynamic in terms of day-to-day life in the household. This meant getting Amy out of her room to do five specific things:

1. Allow her mother in to help clean the room
2. Start looking after her hygiene daily
3. Spend more time downstairs out of her room
4. Introduce some time with her siblings by having meals together
5. Reduce the time she spent on her devices

Stage 2 was split into three distinct steps.

Step 1 – Open Door Policy

Sandra introduced Max into her conversations with Amy. These conversations were on many different levels and through different media. Initially Max would message Amy separately, sending her pictures of what he was up to during the day when he was out at work. The idea was that, as this interaction was non-judgemental and not contentious, it would make it easier to expand the conversation and regain Amy's trust.

This tactic worked really well as it allowed Amy to feel comfortable enough to open her door. It was only a few inches at first but at least her mother could hold her hand as they spoke. Over a few days the door opened wider and wider until it was fully open and Sandra and Amy were sitting on the floor together talking, laughing, drawing, doing word searches, sudoku puzzles, and even board games.

Picture 1. A Tactical Move

This was a beautiful breakthrough. The aim was to start incorporating Amy back into the day-to-day life of the household and most importantly re-introduce her into what was going on at home, and to feel comfortable seeing her siblings walk past her and not want or need anything from her but just be there.

We then got Max to start doing the same thing, which worked very well. When he came home from work he would take over from Sandra and sit down on the floor with Amy. They would just either sit silently or he would read a newspaper while she doodled in a book. It took some time for Amy to get used to her father being there, but very slowly they started doing similar activities to those Amy did with her mother. Over time they managed to persuade Amy to go downstairs to sit in the living room for a couple of hours and watch a programme. That had a wonderful and positive effect and changed their family life completely. For nearly two years there had been no interaction with Amy at all, so this was an amazing turnaround for the entire family.

Step 2 – Elephant Goals

This next step involved breaking down the fundamental issues for Amy's experience of COVID and lockdown. Via Sandra and Max we addressed her fear of COVID, her fears of attending school, and thoughts and feelings towards her friendship groups. We worked on her reasoning for isolation, the fear, and the hate she felt for herself and the people around her.

We needed to reframe what had happened to Amy, identify what was currently going on for her and how she wanted to progress, by visualising goals and creating short-term intermediate targets. The small manageable steps were less daunting for Amy, allowing her to feel each step was achievable. Quite uncharacteristically, Amy agreed to actual deadlines to achieve those individual steps.

We made it fun by introducing the saying "How do you eat an elephant? One bite at a time," as a reminder to break the task down into small steps. We also gave her another analogy, which was "How do you build a wall? One brick at a time!" However, Amy didn't like that one as much and preferred the elephant analogy. She said she would never want to harm, let alone eat, an elephant, but understood the concept. Amy loved this idea and had never heard of it before. It gave her real clarity, purpose and a mental picture of how she could steadily overcome the huge barriers she faced.

Each one of the steps Amy completed gave her immense satisfaction. She found it easier to imagine achieving her goals and even began to look forward to each challenge put in front of her.

We reset her beliefs around friendships, online usage, social media, influencers, family, school, Amy's past, where she was presently and finally, her future.

Step 3 – Fun Family Time
This was getting Amy back into the different parts of the house, whether it was showering or being downstairs eating dinner with the family or watching TV together. During this time Amy responded well to being re-introduced to her siblings and when they watched TV, it didn't matter what the programme was, it was Amy's choice at first. As this became "normal", we introduced suggestions from each family member on what to watch next, so they all had turns to choose. This was an important step as it allowed Amy the time she needed to relearn to adapt and cope with other ideas and suggestions. This was done in the family setting so Amy could create new relationships with trust, safety, tolerance and resilience.

Stage 3 – Get Out!

This was to help Amy get out of the house and integrate with the outside world in a safe and sustainable way.

We re-introduced Amy's best friend from two years prior in a gentle and controlled manner. We carefully choreographed the get-togethers to maximise enjoyment and minimise anxiety and judgement. It started with a cinema trip, then a restaurant, and other meet-ups were slowly added into the equation over time.

Everything we did was based on the entire family's wellbeing, driven by what we knew would be safe for Amy. It was a carefully constructed strategy and needed to be implemented with precision. The best thing about this stage was that Amy fully bought in to what we were doing to re-introduce her into life in 2022.

We re-introduced Amy back into school beginning with one hour per day and increasing that on a week-by-week basis. It increased by an hour or two depending on how she felt. By the end of week six, Amy was nearly back to a full school day. She was working with specific teachers and not within a class of students for the time being. This was so we could re-engage Amy to just go through the school gates. The idea was for Amy to be in a position to make a full return to school the following year, from September 2022. Amy, her parents and the school agreed the reachable targets for Amy's GCSEs, and that she would aim to complete them in one year rather than the usual two.

Conclusion

It took us nine months of intense effort to take Amy from being a recluse, in hibernation and noncommunicative, with severe emotional, mental and physical issues, to being a confident, strong, resilient, self-sustainable and happy teen with dreams, targets and goals she wanted to achieve. We found a solution to the two years she thought she had lost regarding her GCSEs, by agreeing to complete them in one year with the help of the school, some home tutoring, and agreement from Amy that she would turn up to school and take crash courses in some of the subjects to catch up.

By the beginning of the summer in 2022, Amy had regained the confidence and light-hearted spirit of the girl she had been a few years earlier. The previous three years had been incredibly difficult for the whole family. They emerged stronger, resilient and with a very different idea of what life meant as a family. The relationships between each of them individually had strengthened too. Amy passed all her GCSEs with good grades and had just completed the first year of her A levels. She was certainly moving forward with positive intention and focus.

Amy deleted all the social media apps from her smartphone and all other devices. She now only used text messaging to contact her friends and family. Amy's friends now knew to invite her to events or get-togethers by sending her text messages, and this system worked perfectly. There were strict rules about screen usage for the two younger children as they grew into teenagers themselves. Sandra and Max were adamant they would not repeat the mistakes they made with Amy. They would use all the lessons learnt, and all the parent-coaching skills developed over the past year and put them into active use. They also had a few Jedi mind tricks I taught them for difficult situations.

Amy was now in a much healthier space mentally, physically and emotionally. Her siblings were also in a better place and were ecstatic that they were able to play a part in the transformation of their older sister. Sandra and Max were relieved to have their daughter back and were happily building a new fun-filled future with their family.

It is important to point out that it took incredible strength and determination from each family member to make the sacrifices and changes required to get themselves back on track. Without a carefully constructed strategy, and remarkable resilience and focus, it wouldn't have been possible to turn this complicated and crippling situation around.

Each strategy is tailored to the individual, their family, and their specific circumstances. The way the strategy is implemented is different nearly every time, and different levers need to be pulled to change direction with positive effect. We always aim to move forward with purpose and the highest positive intention, which is what we did with Amy and her family.

If you would like to know more about becoming a parent-coach, scan the QR code below for the Rebel Insights page at www.RebelTherapies.com where you can find various downloadable information sheets and top tips which are mentioned in this book.

Chapter 7

Game On!

Gaming can be so much fun! I remember when I was given an arcade game called Astro Wars by my parents for my 12th birthday – it was unreal. It was one of the best games on the market at the time and I remember being completely fixated on it. I couldn't wait to get home after school and play what now seems like a very basic game, but it was just amazing … the escapism, the fun, the lights, the noise and the graphics were all brilliant.

Picture 1. Astro Wars Arcade Game 1982

So, I completely get it … I understand the intense thrill of completing each level, getting better, faster, growing my skills and becoming smarter at the game. But even though I had this fantastic game, it didn't take up all my time. There was no Wi-Fi back in the 1980s. I couldn't connect with others and play at the same time, day or night. It was just me and the game, and after a certain point I would stop playing. It wasn't that I was told to stop by my parents or my older brothers, it was just that I had had enough, and I wanted to do something else.

Back in those dark ages it felt as if there was more freedom and so much more we could do. That freedom gave us licence to go out on our own to meet up in the playground below our block of flats and play with other children of different ages ranging from 5 to 18, and we all had a natural space in the playground.

We would jump on the apparatus, the swings or the roundabout, or climb a wall, ride a bike, or play games in the cube, which was basically a small football pitch. It was so small you couldn't even call it a 5-a-side pitch, but it was good enough for us to play football and basketball, and all the other sports that we dreamed up in there. We also played "British Bulldog", a chasing game that involved crazy rough and tumble play. We didn't know it at the time but this creative physical play was essential for our growth, social interaction, and moderation of behaviour.

It taught us to understand and negotiate the different personalities among the different age groups and cultural backgrounds. It taught us about the pleasures and pitfalls of playing with different kids, learning to stick up for ourselves, sometimes doing stupid things and learning from the consequences. The games might have looked chaotic, but there was an order in that playground, and we were not immune from being told off by other kids for doing something stupid, or on the flip side, being integrated into games with older children, because they realised the value of such inclusion. I remember those times with joy and gratitude. They helped shape the person I am now.

That was in the days before the internet and smartphones, even before the real growth in personal computers like the ZX

Spectrum, Amstrad, and the BBC 128K. The only digital games you could play were at amusement parks, or on a slot machine if you were in a pub, so they weren't readily accessible. This allowed children to have a life which was more physically play-based and exploratory.

My children are fascinated by the stories I tell them about my smartphone-free childhood. These are real stories about how I grew up with my brothers, and mixed with a whole bunch of different people in our block of flats in central London. My children quite often tell me that they wish they could go back in time and have a childhood like mine, that they could experience what I did without any of the technology that exists today. One of the things my children mention is that back in those days, between the 1970s and the end of the1990s, we weren't being watched … we could get away with so much more. Nobody was videoing us, there were very few photos being taken, and CCTV didn't really exist, at least not to the extent it does now. That made for a physically riskier and more exploratory lifestyle, and it also meant that you could just be silly and do stuff without it being posted all over the internet. No one could really shame you because we were all doing the same crazy stuff. People could tell stories about you, but it would only be in a very small circle – the reach would be so limited that it would hardly impact us. However, decades have passed, and technology has evolved. We find ourselves in a highly tech-focused society where people even post pictures of their coffee, smoothie, or their brunch for anyone to see online. But how often do we ask, "Who actually cares?" I would argue that we have stealthily been programmed to become slaves to technology. We now have tech telling us when to stand, sit or walk, instructing us via digital watches and smartphones. Are you being controlled by beeps, dings, and notifications? Who's in control?

I want to stress at this point that I am not saying all tech is bad. We have the amazing capability to communicate instantly with each other no matter where we are in the world. We can go online and search for information, we can do video calls with friends and run our businesses from anywhere. We can reach out to family on the other side of the world who we might otherwise have talked to once every few years. We can now speak to them every day for pretty much zero cost and it's wonderful – it truly is. However, there are some pitfalls. Those pitfalls come in the form of bad actors, people and groups that pull your attention into the online digital world at the expense of your experience of the real world. Technology is now being developed with a high level of addictive trigger points, which lure us in until we're hooked. This has been done insidiously since the early 2010s, which is why the unsuspecting population don't seem to see or feel that it's a problem. The gaming industry is part of this problem – whether they've deliberately created it or not.

The gaming industry worldwide makes billions of pounds a year from the sale of their games, add-ons and new versions of the same game. I remember the countless year-upon-year EA Sports FIFA launches which cost me hundreds of pounds. It was "essential" for my son to have the newest version each year, for the new players and upgrade in graphics and functionality.

The games have become more life-like, technically better, with greater complexity, and the graphics are so good that you can't help but be drawn in. Especially for a young person, it's magical. The ability to go online, join a group of people with a similar mindset and disappear from the real world is immensely appealing. Entering this incredibly imaginative and detailed online extravaganza is like digital crack cocaine. Once you start it's terribly hard to jump off. The games immerse you in a world of lights, noise and exhilarating action that smashes your brain with dopamine and causes levels of excitement that are difficult to achieve in the real world.

The highs when playing these games are incredibly high, especially when you're online and fully immersed, and then the lows are incredibly low when coming off the games, perhaps being forced off by your parents. Of the parents I've worked with, over

90% have told me their children show frustration and aggressive behaviour if asked to stop playing, for whatever reason. Some have explained that their children would play for hours if uninterrupted, without a toilet break, or food and water. It's a serious problem for a very high proportion of the parents I work with.

While there are many internal and external reasons why children play these games, the main one is quite simply that playing them is great fun and they are highly addictive. The amount of time children spend on them needs adult moderation. I find myself torn when I say the word "moderation" because I think back to when I was a teenager, and I know that if I had the ability back then to play the types of games that are available now, I too would want to be online and playing for as long as possible.

I too would be a frustrated teenager if I was told I had to moderate, to balance time spent between playing games, doing homework, going to school or getting more sleep. However, one of the most important things that any young person must learn is that there are boundaries we need to adopt to have a healthy balance in our lives. I've highlighted the topic of boundaries all the way through this book and how crucial they are for the wellbeing of young people.

I've had a lot of parents, teachers and guardians reach out to me, asking about the addictive nature of these games and the real-life problems that online gaming causes for the children in their care. There needs to be more guidance for caregivers, which outlines best practices when introducing technology, particularly gaming, smartphones and tablets, to our children. I would suggest the guidelines include:

- Education – teaching children the benefits of balance and moderation.
- Boundaries – creating a contract which is agreed by all parties, where usage limits are clearly defined and consistently upheld.

- Self-examination – ensuring that carers role model "good" tech usage.

It's all well and good having people say here are five or seven or ten tips you can use when regulating your children's time spent online gaming; however, it's not that simple, because each family unit is different. The point is that parents and guardians need resources freely available to them, illustrating what *"good"* in their household could look like. These resources would indicate how and when it is best to introduce technology to children at different age groups, from newborn to 18. The parents I work with are crying out for clear guidelines on how to introduce and manage technology in an empathetic and justifiable way. They want to know how to do this in a non-aggressive, non-intrusive setting, learning techniques to coach their children. It is also important that the parents demonstrate their own ability to implement rationally thought-out boundaries with their own tech usage.

Gaming is one of the biggest household frustrations across the world,[1] and in this next case study, I will tell you about a teenager and his gaming addiction, and why his parents were so desperate for any help whatsoever.

Alex's parents, Bob and Helen, were put in touch with me through one of our mutual friends. It was initially Bob who I spoke to on a Zoom call. Bob's starting comment to me was this:

> *"My son spends too much time playing games online, doesn't get enough sleep, is a stroppy teenager, and trying to get through to him is like talking to a brick wall, he's failing at school, and if he doesn't change then his teachers think he'll fail his course."*

Bob mentioned that he had been told I was *"The Fixer"*, something he called me numerous times over the next few months. Apparently, I could fix any situation regarding a person's addiction to screens. That was very flattering. However, I did make it clear to him that I could only help change beliefs and behaviours regarding screen addiction *if the person with the addiction wanted to change.* There was an additional caveat; the person would need to acknowledge that they had a problem, agree fully with the process and want to take drastic, and at times, difficult action to make that change a reality. I also made it very clear that Bob's intention for Alex needed to be pure.

I explained to Bob that for Alex to identify and critically analyse what was happening in his life – to understand the drive, the desire and need to be online playing games despite the detriment to his wellbeing – it absolutely had to be Alex's choice.

I have helped others in the space of online gaming addiction before, and must highlight that each person's reasoning, reality, and way of coping with what's happening in the outside world (the real world) in relation to what is happening in the online world is very different. Every one of these situations has its nuances.

The only way to help Alex was to ensure that his parents were open and honest with him. Any interaction with me would need to be agreed upfront by Alex, Bob and Helen. They, themselves needed to have that initial conversation with Alex to explain why they wanted an intervention, and that they were going to introduce a coach. The reason was to help him get through his year at college and to help him amend his behaviour in relation to screens, gaming and everything that went with it.

I made it clear that I would not get involved unless that agreement had been made within the family. To help Bob achieve this, I gave him some pointers in how he could approach Alex and how he might want to frame this "intervention".

Bob told me that he and Helen spoke to Alex and that the conversation didn't go very well. Alex believed that his parents were trying to control him, and he found it very upsetting. Alex didn't think he had any problems … he said he was just being a normal teenager, and that he didn't need them to get him a coach to help him change his behaviours.

In my experience, this type of response is quite normal when we challenge our teenagers' behaviours. From their point of view, they're just getting on with their lives and doing what they feel is normal, no different to other teenagers and their friends. To change a young person's thought process, so that they understand there is an issue, takes careful discussion, patience, and putting together "a cunning plan" as Baldrick[2] often said.

When Bob told me that Alex was not open to the suggestion of a coach, I asked him to adopt a slightly different approach, which was to gently ask questions about how things were going with his college work, highlighting the fact that his tutors had been in touch to explain that Alex was falling asleep in class, and that his attention span was extremely low. They had commented that his interaction during the lessons was poor, and that his work was not at the standard required to pass the course. If that continued, Alex would be kicked off the course before the end of the academic year and not be able to progress to the next level, which was where he wanted to be.

The new approach also involved explaining how a coach would be able to identify areas where Alex could introduce techniques into his daily routine to help him reach his goals. This would help him stay on his course, create a more efficient work ethic, and enable Alex to reach his goal of getting to that next level.

Additionally, I would look at the external factors associated with what was happening in his life, how they impacted him, and what he could do to course correct. For the intervention to succeed, it was critical that Alex bought into this approach and took personal responsibility for his actions.

We needed to make sure that Alex understood the seriousness of his mum and dad's decision to invest in a coach. It was important that he recognised he would need to cut down on some of the activities that were interfering with his goals.

I had a strange feeling that there was something amiss with Bob's explanation of the conversation he and Helen had with Alex, so I delved into the details. Bob admitted that he had made a "slight error of judgement". Helen had not been involved in the conversation; it was only between Bob and Alex. Bob explained that he had approached Alex while he was online and in the middle of a gaming session with his friends. This was absolutely the worst possible time to have such an important conversation. It was critical for Bob and Helen that they chose the timing of their next conversation carefully if they hoped to achieve their desired outcome, as timing is an art.

I also explained to Bob that we needed to approach Alex in the most effective and empathetic way possible. To reach the best outcome in this situation, it meant Helen, not Bob, should be the one to have this second and crucial conversation with Alex. Helen knew how to approach Alex in a gentler way, which was less aggressive, less judgemental and less intrusive for Alex.

Guess what? It worked. Helen approached Alex while they were "having a nice chat" in the kitchen and explained that there would be incredible benefits if they introduced him to a coach, and that they'd found someone who would really be able to understand Alex. Helen mentioned that I had been helping young people like Alex for years in this exact space, and that I had played semi-professional football in my younger years, knowing this was something that Alex would immediately connect with. It sold Alex the deal as he was a football fanatic, a talented player and a big Southampton fan.

Rapport – May The Force Be With You!

My first meeting with Alex was an interesting one. Alex and his family lived in Surrey, which meant our sessions were conducted through Zoom video calls. I encourage my clients to have their camera on. However, you need to sometimes meet the clients where they are at, and with Alex this meant no camera switched on for the first session – he just wasn't ready for that.

Alex wanted his camera switched off, but he wanted to see me and hear me, and for me to hear him but not see him. From my perspective this was completely fine as it was imperative he was totally comfortable in our first session. If the client feels pressured, they will just close up like a clam, and so the session would be a waste of time, effort and money.

In fact, it was Helen and not Alex that initially joined the first call. Alex had asked Helen to talk to me about the camera question as he didn't feel comfortable enough to ask himself. When I spoke to Helen, the camera was on, and I spotted some stuff on Alex's bookshelf. I could make out that he had a few Star Wars[3] figures – a Stormtrooper and a Mandalorian – as well as a mini football. At that moment I knew I was onto a good thing with Alex, and I would be able to create a fantastic connection, just from what I saw on his shelf.

I was able to establish a positive rapport by pointing out to him that I'd had a sneak peek at his bookshelf, and it looked like he was a Star Wars fan. He heartily agreed and started laughing, saying "you're like Superman" regarding my eyesight. I then tilted my camera and showed him what I had on my bookshelf – my own Star Wars figures. He was so impressed that we easily fell into an enthusiastic discussion about all things Star Wars and what else he liked. It was a fun way for us to build trust and rapport, especially seeing that Alex was a slightly suspicious teenager to begin with.

This is one of the most important phases in all my work with clients. By creating that connection and empathy, we remove barriers, and the client becomes more open in their discussions as they feel a greater level of trust and safety.

The first conversation I had with Alex was a fact-finding mission, with the primary objective being for him to feel comfortable with me and know that he was in a safe space, so he could say whatever he wanted about absolutely anything. My job was to gently provide a positive way through this process, encourage Alex to express his viewpoints, and move towards opening up about his gaming addiction.

The "Three Things" Rule

We started by implementing coping strategies for Alex, for his work commitments at college and personally. Alex explained that he struggled to do his assignments by the set deadlines and had shocking time management. He would always be late with his project work and assignments, as he always left them till just before the deadlines and generally missed them because he had no idea what was due and when. It seemed as if he didn't care. To improve Alex's poor time management, I introduced a timed focus technique that many clients find useful.

I also introduced a simple daily diary for Alex so he could schedule his work more effectively. It was important not to overwhelm Alex, as he was finding it difficult to concentrate on more than one thing at a time.

During the late 1990s my own mentor, Rich, taught me an important technique that he called the "Three Things" rule. Whether it was something personal or business related, the most effective and efficient way to deliver any type of project was to identify and prioritise "Three Things" to work on at any one time. It was a rule he set great store by, and it never let him down. I adopted his "Three Things" rule and it has helped me ever since. I introduced the "Three Things" rule to Alex.

Alex's "Three Things"

Firstly, we scheduled Alex's college work so that he knew exactly what he was behind in, what he had to do on a day-to-day basis, what he had coming up in the following month, and how he would catch up with the outstanding work.

The second thing was to create an environment, a schedule and a strategy that would allow him to focus on doing his work without any other interruptions. This is when I introduced Alex to the 45-minute focus technique.

Thirdly, and most importantly, we ensured that Alex turned up for college, as his high absenteeism was jeopardising his future on the course. For Alex to pass his course he had to turn up for at least 85% of the scheduled course college days. He also had to pass all his coursework and exams with a 75% pass rate.

Alex and I decided the "Three Things" strategy in the first two sessions. My initial aim was to create a level of stability, balance and structure that would provide a solid platform for Alex to build upon. We didn't discuss anything to do with gaming, the late nights, and the 5am finishes until our third session. The most important thing was getting him on the right track without being thrown off his college course – that was our priority.

It was essential that Alex fully committed to this new timetable and strategy. The challenge was for Alex to prove to himself that he was capable and adult enough to do this. The next thing in our sessions was for Alex to choose the amount of time he would spend doing his studies, catching up on his work, and the number of 45-minute focused time slots he would set aside to make that happen. It couldn't be me telling him what to do – the plan had to be drawn up by Alex himself. This activity on its own was a massive breakthrough as it meant Alex had to take responsibility. He had to choose what he thought was reasonable and felt good for him. He made it clear to me that he didn't want to let himself down. Equally, he didn't want to let his parents or his grandparents down.

Additionally, Alex had relationship issues with a number of his college tutors, which was causing huge problems. We spent a lot of time unpacking these college relationship issues. It didn't help that the week we started working together, Alex threw a textbook towards one of his friends, who ducked out of the way, so it hit one of his tutors full in her face, causing a nosebleed. It also didn't help that she was one of the tutors Alex had the most problems with. He was nearly expelled for that; and was given a reprieve only after our desperate intervention with the college. He was skating on extra thin ice and only one more slip-up away from expulsion.

We started by listing all the tutors and all their good and bad points. I then encouraged Alex to be as explicit as he wanted to be, to expel all his frustrations, anger, annoyance, and his stress towards his college work, his tutors, the college, the course, and the people around him.

It became clear that all these areas of his life were intrinsically entangled, and a slight change in one of these finely balanced areas would impact multiple other areas in his life. For instance, if he missed the deadline on one of his projects it negatively impacted how his tutor would treat him in class. This would impact how he would behave in the class and affect other students. His behaviour would sometimes get out of control, so much so that his tutor would send him out of the class. In turn this would impact his immediate learning, and he wouldn't find out what work was coming up, which meant he didn't get to finish the work in the class. The knock-on effect was that his workload would build up to a point where he was overwhelmed and unable to see the light at the end of the tunnel. That would make him frustrated, which would impact his mood and his ability to think clearly when he got home.

In an attempt to reduce the overwhelm of these continuous knock-on effects, Alex would log on to his computer as soon as he got home. There was never a shortage of people online to play with. Alex explained that there were people online 24/7, and it was "so easy to be distracted by it". The gaming provided temporary relief, but the fear of returning to his overwhelming real-world responsibilities only grew. In these moments Alex was caught in a downward spiral.

He would play online all night, often seeing the sunrise, realise he had been up for a little too long, and then would fall asleep from exhaustion. This meant that Alex would miss a day of college, resulting in his main tutor sending an email to his mother, who would then have to prompt Alex to get into college the next day. Alex became stuck in this repetitive pattern. It was important to break the back of Alex's *Groundhog Day*.

Alex committed to implementing between three and four 45-minute focus sessions per day. The main rule Alex would have to follow was that he had no devices next to him, the Wi-Fi was switched off, he'd had sufficient sleep the night before, was focused and committed to doing the work. Our agreement was that Alex would send me a message every day to tell me the number of 45-minute focus sessions he had completed and how he was feeling. At this point we needed regular "ecology checks" to find out how Alex was feeling. If there were elements that needed tweaking, we could address them in a timely fashion.

The turnaround in his study and rapport with his tutors, which happened within four weeks, was phenomenal. While it wasn't the end goal, Alex was certainly moving in the right direction. This was the beginning of what we set out to achieve. It was an excellent step towards positive change for Alex.

Committing to this new schedule, messaging me each day with the number of 45-minute sessions, turning up to college and taking photos of his schedule of work gave Alex confidence – something he had not felt for many years.

When we discussed this in our third session Alex explained he was very surprised by what he could do, and really proud of himself. The one thing that stood out for me was how Alex expressed his appreciation for the positive acknowledgement of his work. His tutors at college praised him for the quality of his work, his commitment, timekeeping and attitude. He also received a lot of praise from his family. This was something that Alex hadn't experienced since he was very young. That's not to say that he didn't get praise from his family, but it was pretty rare. Alex explained that he more commonly got a "telling-off or lecture" from his parents, demanding he step up, do more and not be so lazy, messy and incapable.

I witnessed a massive change in Alex's demeanour between our second and fourth sessions. In the second session, which is the first time I saw Alex face to face, he was sitting slumped in his gaming chair talking to me on his iPad, which he kept moving. I could only see the top half of his head, and sometimes just his forehead, the ceiling or the wall. At times he would mumble or grunt, not wanting to be fully committed. However, by the fourth session he was sitting upright, the iPad was on a stand and wasn't moving all over the place, he was very focused, and what surprised me most was at times he would lead the conversation, which was another breakthrough.

One month into this process Alex was progressing very well but still having problems with his sleep patterns. Alex was still missing odd days at college, and it was still causing him problems in catching up on the work missed, which was critical to him passing and graduating to the next level of the course.

The idea of not being online with his mates was triggering Alex's deep-rooted FoMO – his fear of missing out on fun, connectivity and camaraderie, and he was also being pressured by his friends. Helen and Bob had admitted they were not able to control Alex's screen timekeeping, and his sleep patterns continued to be a serious cause of concern.

Unpacking this with Alex took several sessions. Alex didn't want to look like the weak link in his mates' group. He didn't want to look like the one that was conforming to his parents' demands, being told that he had to go to bed at a more reasonable time. He didn't want the mickey being taken out of him by his peer group, which could be so unforgiving in the severity of their comments. He had seen this done to somebody else previously, and that person had eventually dropped out of the peer group, due to the pressure and constant jibes directed at him. For Alex, to be dropped from his mates' group was inconceivable, and something he wouldn't be able to bounce back from. With that in mind, we devised a strategy to reduce the amount of time spent gaming which he considered a reasonable compromise.

We identified two main areas to work on. First, we pinpointed the reasons for playing the game – how he felt about gaming, when and why he did it, and how it elevated his standing within his peer group. The second area was unpacking the strength and depth of his friendship group, and his vulnerabilities within that group.

We highlighted what was important about his gameplay and being online, what would be a reasonable amount of time to be online, and how his friends would react to changes in his game playing pattern. We also discussed how the change would affect his family life, the possible improvement it would have on his sleeping patterns, and the positive domino effect to his college life and work, and how his tutors would perceive those positive changes.

Gameplay

Alex told me that he enjoyed gameplay more than anything else: "It was absolutely fantastic". He mentioned he had a group that would nearly always be online at the same time, and that it would always be fun, as most of the people he played with online were his best friends from school. They had grown up together while being online playing these games, and this had saved them during the COVID lockdowns. Therefore, it was important for Alex not to stop playing completely. Fortunately, neither Alex's parents nor I had suggested this.

It was important for both Helen and Bob to understand that with everything we did there was a balance, a trade-off. This intervention was not to stop Alex from playing his games – it was to reduce the amount of time Alex spent playing games and being online. We needed to help him get a balance between gaming and the other parts of his life. As we explored this, we tried different techniques to highlight the areas of Alex's life that were being harmed by his gameplay.

This part of the process was key. Alex himself identified the areas that were being sabotaged. Before Alex could make changes, he had to first understand the negative consequences his actions were having, and their impact on his ecosystem.

By identifying these negative consequences Alex was for the first time able to see, understand and reflect on the effects his actions were having on him. This enabled him to make more informed, helpful choices. Alex demonstrated that he was now ready to create an action plan to reduce his gaming time.

It took us several sessions to fully firm up the strategy that Alex would use. It had to be Alex's choice, and it had to be done within a time frame he himself had set. This meant that he fully owned the process and was responsible and accountable for it. It was essential for Alex to feel empowered and be in charge of his own destiny.

The reduction of game time was carefully controlled for several reasons. It allowed Alex to feel comfortable about his choice and enabled him to feel that he was in total control of what he was doing. It familiarised his friends with the idea that Alex would be spending less time on the game. Without any sudden and drastic changes, his friends accepted the change without any of the drama Alex had been worried about. However, the time he did spend online, which was still a decent amount, was quality, committed, and a lot of fun.

The positive impact on Alex's sleeping patterns was amazing. Instead of going to bed around 2am and on some occasions several hours later, he got to bed somewhere between 11:30pm and 1am. There were times when Alex slipped from his routine and ended up playing until sunrise. Those hiccups were necessary and valuable to his learning because they served as a reminder of the consequences of getting out of balance.

Change Appreciated

Bob and Helen noticed the ongoing change that was taking place with Alex. They witnessed the return of his energy, light-heartedness and his fun, happy personality. During our time together, Alex confided that he also enjoyed baking, and that he used to bake cakes with his younger sister. However, that hadn't happened for several years. Due to Alex's gaming addiction, he had let that go. Since we started working together, and especially during the last couple of months, Alex started baking again to the delight of his family, especially his sister, as she loved spending time baking with him.

The strategies Alex adopted also included introducing some new and old interests into his life. Along with the baking sessions with his sister, the family movie night was re-introduced. He was spending time playing cards with his grandparents again, and reading a book for fun like he used to.

The transformation for Alex and his family during that six-month period was life-changing. It enabled Alex to label and manage his addiction to gaming and the online world. He adopted new techniques to control his gaming desires, and when, how and why he chose to play. Alex now considered his gaming as a fun hobby and maintained his real-world friendships and online playing groups. This intervention completely turned Alex's life around – in terms of his college life, his quality of work, his relationships with his tutors, and his standing within the college community. He improved his sleeping habits and felt more energised, focused and peaceful.

In our final session Alex was keen to highlight that he really appreciated his parents' intervention. Alex explained that he couldn't understand or appreciate where he was before the intervention as he "just fell into a behaviour" that was too difficult to pull back from. Approaching Alex from a non-judgemental, non-confrontational perspective, and listening to him, allowed him to feel safe to express his thoughts and helped him take radical action. Alex said that while going through the process it seemed drastic at times, yet when he looked back at it, it seemed so simple. Alex told me he felt that he will always be in debt to his parents for encouraging him "to see the light".

There are countless children like Alex, both male and female, who are lost in the online world and who need, and would most likely appreciate, an intervention of the sort Alex had.

Screen addiction is a pandemic and needs to be addressed. Interventions like the one Alex experienced are definitely required. There is always help out there for those who ask for it. One of my favourite quotes is from Harry Potter, wherein Professor Dumbledore says to Harry:

> *"Help will always be given at Hogwarts to those who ask for it."*[4]

In this case, I would like to slightly amend that quote and say that help will always be given at Rebel Therapies for those who seek it. Do not suffer in silence. Take massive action and create that intervention for your children if you notice something amiss.

> *"Understanding is the first step to acceptance, and only with acceptance can there be recovery."*[5]

If you would like to know more about becoming a parent-coach, scan the QR code below for the Rebel Insights page at www.RebelTherapies.com where you can find various downloadable information sheets and top tips which are mentioned in this book.

Conclusion

In the introduction to this book, I talked about the moment I "woke up" and started to change my behaviour regarding the use of screens, particularly my smartphone. When you read the case studies detailed in this book, could you identify a "wake up" moment for yourself?

I wrote this book to help raise awareness of how our children are drawn to devices, not just because of their addictive nature but also because of the various ways parents and guardians are struggling to meet the needs of their children in our fast-changing contemporary society. In all of these case studies, the most important lesson learnt by the parents is that they felt they neglected their children by not being fully present, allowing their children to turn to devices as a parental substitute.

These parents experienced great anxiety and pain as a result due to their lack of awareness. When they realised what a precarious place they were in, they all decided on an intervention as they couldn't cope with the situation a moment longer.

The intervention with these parents enabled them to grow their awareness and implement techniques which transformed both their lives and the lives of their children. It strengthened their relationships and allowed them to create safe spaces where they could discuss whatever they wanted in a non-judgemental and non-aggressive way. This enabled them to move forward with renewed positive connection.

They have become parent-coaches, who are now better equipped to parent in an ever-evolving, technologically driven world, using super-charged strategies and techniques to maintain focus and protect their priorities.

Another topic which regularly came up in my discussions with these parents was the constant availability of content to watch on a device and how easy these devices were to carry around, making them harder to monitor and manage. Most parents I spoke to mentioned that their children expected to have access to these devices wherever they were. Do we really need a smartphone/ iPad/ tablet dock on the pram, or a colourful stand so that we can prop up the devices in front of our children whether we're in a café, in the car, in the bath, or at the dinner table?

How much exposure to technology is okay for our children, and when does it become too much and turn them into "sheep", following mindless content on these devices.

Consider these reflection points:

- At what point do we say this is not in the best interests of our children?
- Who helps us to say, "STOP USING THESE DEVICES!"?
- When and how do we get our children to look up and just see the world through their own eyes and not through the screen?
- When do we adults wake up, smell the coffee, and acknowledge the damage **we** are causing our younger generations?

It's time to Rebel against the designs of Mark Zuckerberg (META, previously known as Facebook), Sundar Pichai (Alphabet Inc, including Google) and Elon Musk (X, previously known as Twitter), and do something that is for the mental, physical and emotional betterment of our children, because those entrepreneurs do not subscribe to the same wellbeing mindset as you and I. Their primary focus is to entice you onto their platforms to grab, trap, hold and sell your attention to advertisers.

We need to create a global intervention for the wellbeing of our children before it we resemble the tragic dystopia depicted in George Orwell's *1984*.

I fear we are at a precipice right now. Given the immense power of AI (Artificial Intelligence)[1] and the immeasurable impact it will have on global society over the coming years, if we don't change our trajectory then we could, like lemmings, follow each other off that cliff to a desperate end.

Are we inventing technology so powerful that it eventually controls what we feel, see, do, and how we react, thus shaping us, taking away our free will, changing our behaviour and rewiring our brains?

I am frightened by the way we as a society are allowing our children to grow in this current habitat, and about what might happen to them through our inaction and neglect. There are elections, wars and everyday events being manipulated through deletion, distortion, generalisation, misinformation and lies on social media. Even when some of those mistruths are called out, it doesn't stop the false messages being absorbed into people's minds, and those messages are impacting the rationality of people's behaviour.

We are being told when to stand, sit, exercise, how to breathe a certain way, take more steps, eat, and drink. How have we lost the ability to do these seemingly instinctive things without being prompted by an app on our smartphones or smart watches? The ability to do the simplest things is being carefully stripped from us. We need to stand up and shout from the rooftops, "THIS IS NOT OKAY!" Something has to change.

Take action now!

We need our politicians to step up and make some seriously tough decisions which will not be universally popular. They need to introduce robust regulations that force the tech companies to deliver humane technology.[2] It is not right that people's eyeballs are being farmed to fill the treasure chests of a few tech billionaires.

Tristan Harris from the Centre of Humane Technology – in my opinion the world's leading authority in this space – is seeking to hold the billionaire owners of tech giants and our politicians to account, demanding of them clearly defined regulations to protect our society.

Yet we still march like zombies into oblivion, not listening to the facts, the science that tells us the usage of these devices, and specifically the technology that is housed within them, is harmful to us. In my opinion, we need to take deliberate steps to create a new future, by helping people understand how to balance the positive and negative aspects of technology. At the same time, we need to introduce humane tech to our young in a staged and careful way, creating a more caring and responsible world. Do you think that is too much to ask for?

There is some hope out there. Action groups like Smartphone Free Childhood among others are popping up all over the world, demanding a change in how we adopt mobile device driven technology. However, these groups are currently fragmented. If we can bring them together with a common and focused strategy, we might be able to tip the balance to make a real difference for our children.

A Moment to Breathe

Why not take a moment to breathe and think before you introduce technology to your children? Consider the questions below before taking that next step towards the technology abyss:

- What did we as a society do before these devices were readily available?
    - How did we connect with our children?
    - What games did we play with them?
    - How did we keep them entertained?
    - How did they learn to entertain themselves?
- What do our children want from us now?
- What else can we do?

I remember having a bucket full of toy cars and soldiers that I would play with all through my childhood. I created endless adventures for my toys and my imagination took me to many thrilling places. I also played music on my ancient cassette player, listening to the latest sounds from the 70's and 80's after recording the BBC Radio 1 Top 40 charts on Sunday afternoon.

The lengths we had to go to in order to find new things to do was at times challenging and at other times refreshing. We had to be resourceful, research, and problem solve – key skills that many employers look for in young jobseekers. But these skills are not being fully developed in young people, because it's easy now to find all the answers with a few clicks on our devices. The art of identifying issues, problem solving and finding creative solutions is being eroded.

So, where do we go from here? Do we ban these devices? This is a topic of serious conversation in most Western societies. Banning smartphones for under 16s; is this where we want to be? Is this the solution? I don't think so. I think we go backwards by banning. I believe it just puts more pressure on already struggling parents and doesn't solve the underlying issues. We need to put strategies and techniques in place about how to introduce technology to our young and educate them in how to grow safely with technology. We need to ask: Have we outgrown our schooling / education system? Are we teaching our children the right skills, passing on appropriate knowledge to survive in their fast-changing world?

I believe that there must be a complete shake-up in how we educate our children. We need to teach them the basics about life, and practical skills to help them navigate the 21st century. We need to teach them how to engage with technology, which can be done by up-skilling parents and teachers with knowledge and techniques to help create a more humane world.

Find Out More

To find out more about the topics covered in this book and becoming a parent-coach, I offer three main resources:

1. Combat Screen Addiction Programme

If you would like to become a parent/teacher/guardian coach, join us on our Combat Screen Addiction Programme.

The course offers practical solutions and support for parents and caregivers who want to tackle screen addiction head-on.

The programmes are designed not just to reduce screen time, but to promote long-lasting behavioural change and help families reconnect in deeper, more meaningful ways. They also offer access to a community of like-minded people who want to make a difference.

We are focused on creating a happier, healthier, more inclusive world for everyone, including our children and future generations to come!

www.rebeltherapies.com/course-booking

If you want to learn more about how to take back control of your family's screen habits, Rebel Therapies offers a range of resources to help parents and caregivers navigate the digital age.

2. Rebel Insights

Here you can find downloadable information sheets about the techniques and tips set out in the book. We will update Rebel Insights regularly to help you navigate the jungle that is the online world.

There is so much changing so quickly in this space that we would like to keep you informed as soon as we become aware of new developments.

3. Rebel to Rebel

Help on a 1-2-1 basis: If you think your family could benefit from an intervention similar to these case studies, please reach out to us via our contact form at the following address:

www.RebelTherapies.com/therapies

Technology keeps evolving and so we need to be agile in the way we manage our wider lives. We need to be mindful and curious about its evolution, and as such Rebel Therapies will be creating more content for you to make sense of it and consider how it will affect us in the years to come.

Please join me and my team at www.RebelTherapies.com as we continue to navigate and course correct, so we can help both our children and ourselves to create a fulfilling and humane future intertwined with technology.

End Notes

For a comprehensive list of books consulted in the research of this book, please visit www.RebelTherapies.com/ScreenAddict/bibliography.

Acknowledgments

[1] Weitz, Chris & Gilroy, Tony. (2016). *Rogue One: A Star Wars Story,* Disney Studios

Introduction

[1] Watson, Stephanie. (18 April 2024) *Dopamine: The Pathway to Pleasure,* Harvard Medical School (https://www.health.harvard.edu/mind-and-mood/dopamine-the-pathway-to-pleasure)

Chapter 1 – How Young is Too Young?

Picture 1. Illustration of Sarah's Penguin and Portable Light

[1] Gallo, Amy. (2 January 2024) *What is Active Listening,* Harvard Business Review (https://hbr.org/2024/01/what-is-active-listening)

Chapter 2 – The Nude Predator!

[1] https://dictionary.cambridge.org/dictionary/english/bad-actor

Picture 1. Emma's Instagram

Picture 2. Swallow Me Up

[2] Barker, Eric. (7 June 2016) *This Is The Best Way to Overcome Fear of Missing Out,* Time.com (https://time.com/4358140/overcome-fomo/)
[3] Payne, Steve. (2020) Academy of Coaching & Training (https://www.taoct.uk/whatisnlp)

Chapter 3 – Gamification

[1] Barney, Nick. (2023) *gamification,* TechTarget.com (https://www.techtarget.com/searchhrsoftware/definition/gamification)
Picture 1. Coins, Credits, Bucks
[2] Lembke, Dr. Anna. (2021) *Dopamine Nation*, Headline
Picture 2. Daylight Robbery!

Chapter 4 – Online Babysitter

[1] Haidt, Jonathan. (2024) *The Anxious Generation,* Penguin Books
[2] Higa, G.S.V., Francis-Oliveira, J., Carlos-Lima, E. *et al.* (5 December 2022) *5-HT-dependent synaptic plasticity of the prefrontal cortex in postnatal development,* Nature.com (https://doi.org/10.1038/s41598-022-23767-9)
[3] Ramis, Harold and Rubin, Danny. (1993) *Groundhog Day,* Columbia Pictures
[4] Payne, Steve. (2020) *NLP Practitioner,* Academy of Coaching & Training
Pictures 1, 2 & 3. Munur's Candy Crush Saga Game on iPhone
[5] Labrinth featuring Emeli Sandé, (2012). *Beneath Your Beautiful,* Album: Electronic Earth, Syco

Chapter 5 – Good Nude Bade Nude

Pictures 1 & 2. Snapchat Example
Table 1. DEFCON Levels. Veteran.com, (June 8 2023). https://veteran.com/defcon-levels/
Picture 3. Perfect Body Shapes

Chapter 6 – Lockdown Shutdown!

[1] Parentkind. *School anxiety and refusal,* (https://www.parentkind.org.uk/for-parents/health-and-wellbeing/school-anxiety-and-refusal#)
Picture 1. A Tactical Move

Chapter 7 – Game On!

Picture 1. Astro Wars Arcade Game 1982

[1] Opera Limited. (2 June 2022) *Gamer rage is more than memes: Opera GX presents its first Rage Report with key insights on US and UK gamers' daily frustrations*, PR Newswire https://www.prnewswire.com/news-releases/gamer-rage-is-more-than-memes-opera-gx-presents-its-first-rage-report-with-key-insights-on-us-and-uk-gamers-daily-frustrations-301560462.html

[2] Curtis, Richard & Atkinson, Rowan. (1983) *Blackadder "The Foretelling"*, BBC1

[3] Lucas, George. (1977) *Star Wars - A New Hope,* 20th Century Fox

[4] Rowling, J. K. (1998) *Harry Potter and the Chamber of Secrets,* Bloomsbury (UK)

[5] Rowling, J. K. (2000) *Harry Potter and the Goblet of Fire,* Bloomsbury (UK)

Conclusion

[1] Stryker, Cole & Kavlakoglu, Eda. (16 August 2024) *What is artificial intelligence (AI)?*, https://www.ibm.com/topics/artificial-intelligence

[2] 'Humane Technology' - Centre for Humane Technology https://www.humanetech.com/

Personal Reflections

Notes for any thoughts, feelings, questions and comments that have arisen from these case studies…

Printed in Great Britain
by Amazon

61536292R00097